why Shakespeare

why Shakespeare

An Introduction to the Playwright's Art

GERALD M. PINCISS

continuum
NEW YORK • LONDON

2005

The Continuum International Publishing Group Inc
15 East 26 Street, New York, NY 10010

The Continuum International Publishing Group Ltd
The Tower Building, 11 York Road, London SE1 7NX

Printed in the United States of America

Library of Congress Cataloging-in-Publication Data
Pinciss, G. M.
   Why Shakespeare : an introduction to the playwright's art / Gerald M.
Pinciss.
     p. cm.
   Includes bibliographical references and index.
   ISBN 0-8264-1688-8 (hardcover : alk. paper)
   1. Shakespeare, William, 1564–1616—Technique. 2. Drama—Technique.
I. Title.
PR2995.P56   2004
822.3'3—dc22   2004019403

For Lewis Falb

Since my dear soul was mistress of her choice,
And could of men distinguish, her election
Hath sealed thee for herself.

Hamlet (III.ii)

"Because human judgment . . . never becomes infallible and approbation may yet be only . . . prejudice or fashion, it is proper to inquire, by what peculiarities of excellence Shakespeare has gained and kept the favour of his countrymen."

Samuel Johnson, *Preface to Shakespeare*, 1765

CONTENTS

Illustrations may be found between pages 96 and 97.

PREFACE

THIS BOOK IS addressed to those interested in understanding why William Shakespeare is regarded as the most important playwright in the English-speaking theater. The discussion in the following pages requires no broad knowledge or specialized training in English Renaissance literature nor does it presuppose (or provide) a background in the Elizabethan age or in Shakespeare's England. There are books enough on those subjects.

Why Shakespeare examines in some detail the author's skill in dramatizing a story, developing complex characters, and creating a language that makes his work emotionally and intellectually rewarding. No particular theoretical bias is favored. This book assumes that human nature is universal, remaining fundamentally the same as it was in Shakespeare's day. Since the human condition has not changed in a way that makes the world of Shakespeare's creations alien, the concerns, emotions, values, and personalities of his characters remain recognizable, and their imagined lives reward the attention of a modern theatergoer.

As examples for analyses, the following chapters focus on the dozen or so plays that are most often performed and that are generally regarded as most influential. An intimate familiarity with these texts is not a prerequisite, for the discussion provides all essential information about plot, character, and language.

With the general reader in mind, I have avoided using the specialized vocabulary and technical language of literary analysis, and I have banished literary theory. The few critics who are occasionally cited here have well withstood that most acid of tests, the test of time.

The continued popularity of Shakespeare's work is proof of its enduring ability to speak to new generations. *Why Shakespeare* examines the means by which this writer demonstrates the astonishing ability characteristic of all great works of art: to transcend his own age.

ACKNOWLEDGMENTS

ANYONE ATTEMPTING to write in an informed manner on Shakespeare's work has incurred vast debts. My first experience with many of the plays occurred when I was still in my teens, growing up in a small town north of Boston and not far from Cambridge. A favorite teacher would take me on excursions to the Brattle Street Theater near Harvard, where I first saw performances of such plays as *Henry IV, Parts One and Two* (both for the price of one ticket!) and *Much Ado About Nothing* (set in a Mexican hacienda in the early nineteenth century). Obviously, I have never forgotten these formative experiences. My indebtedness to my teachers and to those who perform the plays began very early and has continued.

The books listed in my notes are an inadequate acknowledgement of what I have learned from those who contributed by their publications to my understanding of Shakespeare's work, theater, and world, as anyone familiar with the scholarship in these subjects will readily perceive. I have absorbed so much from books read over the years that often I can now no longer determine what scholar or critic was the source of a particular insight or piece of information. The bibliography is merely suggestive of those who have been most influential in directly shaping my discussion in these pages.

I am also grateful to my former students. For over thirty years I taught Shakespeare's plays in undergraduate and Masters classes at Hunter College and, for several years, in doctoral seminars at the Graduate Center of The City University of New York. Those decades in the classroom surely taught me, or forced me to learn and discover, more than I would have had I not had to confront those eager, perplexed, and bewildered faces several times a week, rushing to their seats fresh off the bus or out of the depths of the subway. Dealing with their curiosity, confusion, indifference, delight, and, even at times belligerence challenged my pedagogical skills and made my teaching career exciting and rewarding. I was especially fortunate to have a program that allowed me almost exclusively to offer courses on Shakespeare and the drama of the English Renaissance, the literary material that I most enjoyed. I hope that I have conveyed some of that pleasure to those under my tutelage.

To two colleagues I would like to express particular thanks. My former officemate, Professor Marlies Danziger, read this manuscript and saved me from lapses both of content and grammar. As ever, her good judgment and sound reason have greatly improved the text. I am fortunate indeed to enjoy the pleasure of her friendship and the benefit of her counsel. These pages also profited from the criticism and advice of another close colleague, my fellow in Shakespeare studies at Hunter, Professor Irene Dash. And one of the best of my undergraduates, Edilberto Soriano, read my words with becoming modesty. Ruth Wolff, the noted playwright, gave me the benefit of her professional wisdom; I am deeply indebted to her for her careful reading of the text and for her excellent advice. Of course the faults and oversights that remain are solely mine. In addition, I wish to acknowledge the help and guidance of several dear friends. Donald Spoto's counsel, as always, proved indispensable. Elaine Markson, my agent, as well as those in her office, have given me the assurance and support necessary for turning my words into a published text.

Finally, I wish to thank all those dear friends who asked provocative questions, urged me to write, and expressed continuing faith in my efforts. Their intellectual curiosity and genuine eagerness to understand have more than once lifted a flagging spirit. Preeminent in this list are Kenneth J. Rhodes, as well as my sister and brother-in-law, Nancy and Paul Freireich. I would have achieved little without their encouragement and interest. And once again I am fortunate to have as my editor at Continuum, Evander Lomke, who has as in the past proved a sharp-eyed, astute, and sensitive reader. My greatest debt, and the one for which I am most grateful, is acknowledged in the dedication.

1

Introduction

Where should a dramatist begin? Shakespeare must have started with a story. He did not need Aristotle to tell him that plot is the soul of drama. Practical wisdom would have made that clear; and besides, the *Poetics*, the Greek philosopher's little treatise on the art of playwriting, was hardly accessible in sixteenth-century England. But in any case, Shakespeare's interests were not theoretical. He was a practical, commercial writer who aimed to create works for a professional acting company with a ravenous appetite for new material.

For him, the "good story" with dramatic potential could be found in any number of readily available sources—histories (Holinshed's *Chronicles*), classical legends (Ovid's *Metamorphoses*), Greco-Roman biographies (Plutarch's *Lives*), and even contemporary tales (Thomas Lodge's *Rosalynde*), poems (Arthur Brooke's *The Tragical History of Romeus and Juliet*), and plays (*King Leir*).[1] As one of Shakespeare's characters says, "All with me's meet that I can fashion fit": everything is grist for this mill.

The Elizabethans did not discourage such heavy and constant borrowing from multiple sources. To their mind, they were only standing on the shoulders of giants. Since Greece and Rome had already done just about everything worth doing, how could they possibly come up with something totally original? And even if they could, would it be desirable? For writers of the English Renaissance, a creative artist could demonstrate his talent by what he did with what he borrowed. Originality meant showing that they could turn borrowed material into something new by the way it was treated, shaped, developed, and presented. The real contributions of a writer are to be found in the brilliance of a work's organization and presentation, in its language and literary devices, in its ability to engage an audience. Artistic judgment is what determines the uses to which the borrowed material is put, the way it is handled, the response it calls forth. Everything in print may be fair game as a source, but once chosen, the true artist must place his own imprint on it.

With the story line settled, the next matter to resolve concerned the characters, those involved in the events. What kind of people would make these things happen? And to what kind of people do such things happen? For example, what mental attitude or disturbed temperament would motivate someone to want to destroy an innocent young wife like Desdemona or cause her new husband to strangle her on their wedding bed?

Can a dramatist make such a mind-set comprehensible? What must Iago feel, and what has made him feel this way? And then why would Othello so readily believe Iago's false accusation? What are the factors that leave the hero so susceptible to the villain's lies? Why would such an adoring wife as Desdemona prove so unsuccessful in her efforts to reassure her husband of her faithfulness and her love? What combination of factors unites these three inevitably on so disastrous a course? The principals must seem composed of such interlocking strengths and weaknesses, cruelties and insecurities that the tragedy proves unavoidable even though under different circumstances it might easily have been averted. The distinctive personalities, the intense pain and suffering, and the ease with which the outcome could have been different help turn the story into powerful drama.

With a story line in hand and with some sense of what sort of individuals could enact and respond to it, Shakespeare could then turn his energies to making other choices. What kind of language would such people use? Would Iago's manner of expression reflect the same level of inflated rhetoric to describe feminine innocence and beauty as that of the romantic idealist Cassio or the foppish Roderigo?

RODERIGO: ... She's full of most blessed condition.
IAGO: Blessed fig's-end! The wine she drinks is made of grapes.
                                                                        (II.i)

The dialogue and the discourse must reveal the mentality of the speakers. And lovers and villains, clowns and kings, rustics and courtiers must express themselves through words appropriate not only to their individual character traits but also to their social status.

Keeping these elements in mind—the events, the enactors, and their language—Shakespeare must have worked out some overall scheme for the development of the plot. Experience, trial and error, as well as the precedent of the Latin comedies of Terence and Plautus studied as school texts would have taught him the need to shape the arc of the action into what we think of as a five-act structure: introduction, complication, crisis, unraveling, conclusion.[2]

Although act structure was not indicated in performance and often not marked in such manuscripts of other writers as have survived—we have no originals by Shakespeare—the carefully organized sequence of scenes in a Shakespeare play moves the action along so that it reaches a turning point or climax shortly after the opening of Act III, and the denouement or resolution follows directly from that, through Acts IV and V.

Shakespeare wrote rapidly: at one period of his career, he composed two plays a year. He did not always keep minor details in mind—according to some who knew him, his "mind and hand went together" with such ease that there is scarcely "a blot in his papers."[3] But in fact, modern editors have argued that Shakespeare must have thought critically about his work, for he occasionally rewrote and revised.[4] In any case, despite his fluency in composition, he seems to have given a great deal of care to preparing, either on paper or in his mind, a list of the sequence of scenes which would impose the desired shape on the overall action of a play.

In *King Lear*, for example, the climax occurs early in what we regard as Act III, when for the first time the half-mad king, realizing the error of his ways, expresses sympathy with the suffering of others. No sooner has Lear changed than in the brief scene immediately following, the Earl of Gloucester determines that he, too, must change and support his old master, the king. Shakespeare has taken great pains to keep the two story lines in tandem so that the climax in one plot immediately precedes the climax in the other. Lear and Gloucester parallel each other in their development, and the events in the two sequences progress at the same rate. Such precision is hardly accidental; in fact, it demands great planning and great artistry. His choices seem to have been quite consciously made and his effects achieved by deliberate effort.

Another constant to be found in his plays he shares with every truly creative mind: Shakespeare was seldom content merely to repeat himself. Again and again in his works we find him trying out new effects, presenting different ways of dramatizing an old situation, offering his audience something cleverly done in ways they had not seen before. The desire to come up with something varied and new must have been a way of testing his powers as an artist, a direct response to his own creative energies that could turn the mechanics of writing plays into an intellectual and artistic challenge. His dramaturgy would no doubt appeal to audiences, but probably the most rewarding part of his work as a writer involved inventing the new and experimenting with the untried.

This need to innovate, to explore the untried, was a basic element of Shakespeare's creativity, but unlike some writers, Shakespeare's powers were never used in a self-indulgent manner. He set out to delight his audience—"we'll strive to please you every day," Feste proclaims in the last line of *Twelfth Night*—and so his dramaturgy, however experimental, always served that goal.

Indeed, Shakespeare achieved enormous success in the theater, gaining financial prosperity and respect as an artist by his contemporaries. This security and reputation were due in no small measure to the range and variety of his plays. His greatest contemporary, Ben Jonson, never managed to produce a tragedy that found favor with his audiences, and Jonson's brilliance shines brightest only in satiric comedies such as *Volpone*. Shakespeare's ability, however, seems all-encompassing. He specialized in no single genre, and he successfully blended different genres even as he excelled in each.

Shakespeare wrote more plays about the history of England than any other dramatist; in their overall effect, these are sometimes histories-as-comedies (*Henry IV, Part One*), as tragedies (*Richard II*), and even as celebratory pageants (*Henry V*). He created different types of tragedy, adapting material from classical sources (*Julius Caesar; Antony and Cleopatra; Coriolanus*), from native history (*King Lear; Macbeth*), and from Italian love tales (*Romeo and Juliet; Othello*). And when not mining a new vein, he reworked such popularly established stage genres as the revenge tragedy: in *Hamlet*, he provided the ultimate example of this type of play.

The range of his comedies is broad indeed: bourgeois comedy (*Merry Wives of Windsor*); "festive" romantic comedy (*Twelfth Night; Much Ado About Nothing*); pastoral comedy (*As You Like It*); farce (*Comedy of Errors*); tragicomedy (*Troilus and Cressida*); "problem" comedy (*Measure for Measure; All's Well That Ends Well*); and romance (*Cymbeline; The Winter's Tale; The Tempest*). The editors of the first collection of Shakespeare's plays in 1623, known as the *First Folio*, emphasized the fact their colleague was the master of every genre by organizing his works by generic category.

Shakespeare's disregard for the classical unities is also typical; he refuses to be bound by rules or conventions that others would impose—even when they were recommended by such highly regarded artists as Sir Philip Sidney or such learned playwrights as Jonson. Shakespeare may well have been familiar with the commonly accepted (but actually mistaken) notion that according to Aristotle the best works on the stage conform to the three unities: that is, the play presents a single action occurring in one location and spanning no more than twenty-four hours. In fact, Ben Jonson shows us again and again how these restrictions can lead to tightly constructed, compressed, and exciting drama.

But this is hardly true in Shakespeare's case. Twice in his career, Shakespeare demonstrated that he could work comfortably within the pseudo-Aristotelian unities: both *The Comedy of Errors* and *The Tempest* meet all three of the requirements, and they meet them with no obvious signs of strain. Interestingly enough, these two plays were written, respectively, near the beginning and close to the end of Shakespeare's career as a dramatist. Perhaps he intended to demonstrate his familiarity with this principle, although he repeatedly chose not to accept such artificial restrictions.

As Samuel Johnson, one of the greatest of Shakespeare critics, realized, a spectator has no real difficulty in imagining that the action on stage may occur in several different places and over an extended time. Hence, the compression that the unities impose can come at too high a price, foreclosing the scope and power that a longer time sequence or a broader playing field can provide. Final judgment must be based on the effect achieved, and the unities of time and place, as Johnson noted, "have given more trouble to the poet than pleasure to the auditor" or spectator.[5] Once again, in the case of Shakespeare, the desire for variety, range, and innovation carries the day.

This book considers the ways in which Shakespeare's creative genius finds expression in his drama. The openings of his plays often display an astonishing variety of tricks. And in the process, he uses a staggering number of devices to get matters under way, to convey the exposition, to communicate those story details that enable the audience to understand what has preceded this moment on stage and created the initial situation. Then, too, the motivating factors and personalities of the major characters in a Shakespeare play become quickly established in part through his use of character types familiar on the early English stage but whose origins have been lost to us.

Shakespeare carefully orders his scenes so that his very sequencing contributes to the coherence, artistic unity, and design of the work. And he never misleads us; except for one famous instance, he never lies to his audience. In a Shakespeare play, for example, we are very seldom unprepared for the turn of events; as members of the audience, we usually know as much, if not more, than any character on stage. As a consequence, Shakespearean drama unfolds in such a way that we experience not shock and surprise but rather the pleasure of expectations fulfilled. Since our knowledge equals or even exceeds that of anyone on stage, we can derive particular delight in watching how things turn out in just the ways we had anticipated.[6]

Shakespearean blank verse becomes a highly malleable medium of speech, capable of lyric, dramatic, and character-revealing possibilities. How he uses it, how it evolves in his writing, and what effects he achieves with it need to be considered in order to appreciate the range, variety, and subtlety of his dramaturgy. Moreover, Shakespeare mastered not only poetry but also English prose. This, too, requires analysis as well as what Shakespeare does with some of the conventional theatrical elements of his time such as the soliloquy, the eavesdropping scene, the play-within-a-play, the musical interlude, and vocal songs.

Lastly, as is only logical, this book examines the often unsettling ways in which these plays are resolved. The final moments of a Shakespearean drama often raise interesting and troubling questions. For example, should we judge the dying Hamlet, with all his energy, intelligence, sensitivity, and commitment to moral values, a success or a failure? Sometimes more than a touch of irony ties up the strands of the action. Sometimes, too, the ending and the beginning seem related so that the entire play has the feel of completeness about it; the circle closes, the trap snaps shut just when the survivors thought they were free. Perhaps at this point we might even venture to propose some broader comments on the view of life that finds expression in these works.

As advice to readers of the *First Folio,* Shakespeare's editors cautioned: "If you do not like him, surely you are in some manifest danger not to understand him." Their words should be kept in mind, for in the act of participating as witnesses to the world of these plays, we find ourselves entertained like gods, watching from outside with our superior knowledge, breathing the air on Mount Olympus, transported to those incredible heights by the genius of the playwright.

2

Organizing the Story

Transforming one's source material into an effective work for the stage is hardly a simple matter. At what point in the sequence of events will the action begin? Which incidents will be seen by the audience and which will not? In what order will these be presented? The overall design of the drama is established initially by working out the plot and scene sequence. Naturally, no single approach is always appropriate, but in large measure the shaping of the script must reflect the nature and complexity of the story as well as the skill of the writer. As we have noted, Shakespeare chooses material from a wide variety of sources and tries every possible dramatic genre. As a consequence, his plots seem organized in more ways than we might have thought possible.

The simplest and most logical of possible plot structures dramatizes a single story in an unbroken series of actions that builds cumulatively to a climax and resolution. *Julius Caesar* does just this. Shakespeare first establishes the political situation in Rome as well as the nature and varied motives of the conspirators against Caesar. The play then builds toward its climax: after the killing of Caesar at the opening of Act III, the turning point of the action occurs in the very next scene when Antony wins over the Roman populace against Brutus and his cohorts. The battle between the opposing forces fills out the remaining two acts of the play. Shakespeare selected the essential events to dramatize and arranged them in straightforward fashion. The sequence in *Romeo and Juliet* follows a similarly direct and uncomplicated path. The tragedy of Romeo and Juliet unfolds in chronological fashion, and the deaths of Mercutio and Tybalt, which form the turning point of the action, occur at the opening of Act III.

But dramatizing the most simple and direct of tales may require adjustment if the play version seeks to emphasize a particular aspect of the story. *Macbeth*, for example, follows a direct cause-and-effect sequence. The protagonist meets the witches, who plant the notion of murdering the king; Macbeth and his wife then kill Duncan and take his crown; as a consequence, their deed haunts the new king and queen, who are ultimately defeated by the forces of justice and retribution. All this seems uncomplicated, and, in its simplicity, the events could be divided quite easily into the five acts of a play. As the climactic moment and the turning point of the action, the actual stabbing of the king could be expected to take place in Act III. The proposal to seize the throne of Scotland would occupy the Macbeths in Act I; deciding whether, when, and how to kill the king would be determined in Act II; the murder would be enacted in Act III; the remorse and aftereffects of the regicide would be dramatized in Act IV; and the final defeat of the Macbeths would occur in Act V. How logical it all seems.

As it turns out, however, this is not what the playwright actually does. In his treatment of the story line, Shakespeare moves the killing of King Duncan forward to a point much earlier in the action, placing it between the first two scenes of Act II. At the end of II.i, Macbeth follows the bloody dagger of his imagination that will lead him to Duncan's bedchamber. He exits as Lady Macbeth enters and begins the new scene imagining her husband's actions offstage: "He is about it." We do not actually witness the murder of Duncan, in part, no doubt, to help Macbeth retain something of our sympathy for his better nature. But the fact that the killing of the king happens so soon in the sequence of events is totally unexpected.

The speed and surprise make the deed more shocking and dramatically powerful. But the chief advantage to this arrangement is that the audience can turn its attention in the rest of the play to the real subject: dramatizing the cumulative effects of guilt and remorse

that overwhelm the new royal couple. Although the sequence
could hardly be more simple and direct, its treatment is both logical and daring, for it requires Shakespeare to invent ways of dramatizing the mental states of Macbeth and his wife. The playwright
must do more than have them tell us what they are feeling; we must
witness the intensity of their despair in dramatic action. We watch
Macbeth terrorized by his hallucinations, first imagining bloody
daggers in the air and then the corpse of his second victim, Banquo,
seated in his chair. Lady Macbeth reveals both her troubled psyche
and her guilty conscience first by fainting, then by what she says
and does involuntarily in her sleepwalking scene, and finally by her
suicide, which is announced by the cry of women offstage.[7] Shakespeare has found ways of showing us how this tormented couple's
feelings of fear, regret, and despondency are a direct consequence
of their actions. Attempting to enhance their lives and positions,
they have tragically destroyed them, eliminating any love or meaning from their existence. Since the next four acts will stage their
steady, painful descent into nihilism, the event that turns all their
promising beginnings to such bitter emptiness, Duncan's murder,
has been placed appropriately close to the start of the story.

Macbeth seems to happen at a rush. The principals respond to
their opportunities with such alacrity that matters could hardly
turn out other than they have. Time is so compressed, in fact, that
we are unsure for how long Macbeth ruled Scotland. By the conclusion of the play when we become aware of the sorry state of his
kingdom we realize that he has been on the throne for some years.
Yet nothing in the text directly indicates the length of his reign.
Shakespeare often glosses over this issue of the duration of his dramas, of how much time would be required for their enactment,
probably because by his compressing the timeline of the story he
could heighten our sense of its inevitability.

Yet such a rule is not absolute. In *The Winter's Tale* Shakespeare's
unusual plan for this single story-line plot structure comes directly
out of the tale it dramatizes. We may recall that the figure of Time
serves as a Chorus to announce a hiatus between the opening events
and the conclusion of this play. When the action resumes, it is sim-

ply sixteen years later. The interval, marked by Time's soliloquy, divides the two parts of the story, which then moves in reverse sequence. What started so promisingly in Sicilia has ended tragically on the seacoast of Bohemia. Now, after the lapse of time, a new ordering of incidents begins that will retrace the earlier steps but backward, for this later one opens in Bohemia and ends happily in Sicilia.[8] The circle is completed; we are back where we began; the original mood is restored; and all the surviving principals are reunited at the conclusion. The pattern Shakespeare has worked out for the action imposes a sense of rightness or wholeness on the events so that what might in other hands have seemed fragmented or episodic has been shaped into a tightly knit whole.

Much Ado About Nothing is another exception to the general rule of straightforward storytelling. In this case what seems to be the central conflict of the plot gets resolved by the first scene of the second act, much too early in the drama. At that point in the play, the Prince has successfully negotiated Claudio's proposal of marriage to Hero; the Prince's evil brother, John, has tried to make Claudio believe that the Prince wooed Hero for himself; John's deception is revealed; and the young lovers are brought together. The story has a beginning, middle, and happy ending. We need to know nothing more about shy Hero and her even more cautious fiancé, Claudio. And the secondary, witty pair, Beatrice and Benedict, who provided comic contrast, can soon be expected to continue their wit combats as husband and wife. The tale seems just about concluded.

But in fact, in the scene immediately following this joyous resolution, John and his henchmen undertake a new scheme intended "to misuse the Prince, to vex Claudio, to undo Hero, and kill" her father. The playwright needs to wind up the mechanism again if the action is to continue, and so we learn of the villains' second plan, which they expect will cause even greater mischief.

Why does Shakespeare present a first attempt that fails, and that fails so easily and quickly? He surely could have expanded the details involved in Claudio's marriage proposal and in the Prince's role as go-between so that only the second and more serious fraud of John and his agents would be plotted. Then the crisis would occur in Act III, and the remainder of the action would take the form it now has.

Since other concerns must have taken precedence and affected Shakespeare's thinking as he planned the treatment of the story, the real question that needs answering is what are the advantages or benefits of the design he chose? In fact, they are several. First, the ease with which the villains' initial plot is put into operation establishes how nearly everyone in the world of this play can be so readily duped. The first failed scheme establishes both the naïveté of those victimized by John and the sophisticated but overly trusting world in which the action is set. The simplicity of Hero, Claudio, and their family and friends clearly identifies them as vulnerable to the machinations of those who wish them harm.

Moreover, the fact that after failing in their initial effort, John and his followers immediately draw up plans for a second attempt at mischief making proves the determination of the villains to disrupt the happiness of the principal characters. But, as one of the characters says, in both cases the truth is "brought to light."

And by the doubling of the villainy the plotting is more complex, offering us opportunities to appreciate the similarities and differences in the ways these frauds are presented as well as in their consequences. The effect of Shakespeare's design is that *Much Ado About Nothing* has a coherence and richness it would otherwise lack.

In addition to its unexpected plotting, *Much Ado About Nothing* has a broader story line than what we have found in *Macbeth* and even in *The Winter's Tale*. In *Much Ado*, the playwright expands on the personalities of Beatrice and Benedict to enrich the drama with a secondary tale. Although Hero and Claudio, as the principal characters, should have the central roles, Beatrice and Benedict actually attract far more of our attention. Since this older couple is more experienced in the ways of the world, more introspective, and far more witty, they are more engaging than the younger lovers. And with their long-standing antagonism and obstinacy they stand in sharp contrast to the quiet innocence and brief courtship of their friends.

The combativeness of Beatrice and Benedict presents occasions for lively, robust romantic comedy. These two, both quarrelsome and prickly, dominate the stage, and the incidents that involve them form an independent subplot yet remain linked to the main action. To prove the depth of his love for Beatrice, Benedict even defends Hero's reputation by challenging Claudio to a duel. The courtship and marriage of Beatrice and Benedict remain closely tied to the resolution of the Hero–Claudio story.

A slightly more complicated arrangement of incidents is found in *Twelfth Night*. Once again, the story line dramatizes both a main plot and a separate subplot. The main plot involves Viola's love for Orsino, who thinks he loves Olivia, who thinks she loves the disguised Viola. Olivia is also courted not only by the foolish Sir Andrew Aguecheek but also by her steward, Malvolio, whose victimization constitutes the subplot. Ultimately, the arrival of Viola's twin brother, Sebastian, provides the means for clarifying much of the confusion and for resolving matters happily for the major characters.

Shakespeare manages to dramatize these events by alternating scenes so that the incidents can share the same timeline. For example, at the end of Act I, when Viola, in her male disguise, first arrives to declare Orsino's passion for Olivia, Olivia realizes that she is more attracted by the messenger than the message. In an attempt to lure Orsino's agent back for another visit, Olivia sends Malvolio to return a ring she claims the messenger left behind as a token. Olivia has invented this tale simply in the hope of luring her visitor back: "If that the youth will come this way to-morrow,/ I'll give him reasons for't." In the next scene, at the opening of Act II, we meet for the first time Viola's twin and his traveling companion and learn they are on their way to Orsino's court, where we expect they will find Viola. After they exit, Viola and Malvolio enter. He has now caught up with her and insists on her accepting the ring Olivia sent with him. When she is left alone on stage, Viola realizes that Olivia must have been deceived by what she saw.

Now the action returns to life belowstairs in Olivia's household. We are reintroduced to the servants we met earlier in the play.

When Malvolio, arrogant, censorious, and condescending, criticizes their behavior, his manner provides the motive for their plotting to make him look absurd.

This sequence of four scenes provides a sample of Shakespeare's method. By his alternation of story lines involving Orsino, Olivia, Sebastian, and the servants in Olivia's household, Shakespeare interweaves the threads of action and maintains a common time scheme for all of it. None of these incidents will ultimately turn into a separable history except for the gulling of Malvolio; apart from that, all the other events in the plot are a consequence of the confusion caused by Viola's disguise and her love for Orsino.

The tricking of Malvolio, to make him believe that Olivia returns his love, is an entirely coherent, separate action, independent of the incidents involving Viola-Orsino-Olivia-Sebastian. And the Malvolio story is appropriate in the broader context of the play, for it is another example of misguided love and of the effects of self-love. Everything that occurs is related thematically even though the twists and turns of the plot involve different social spheres, different households, and characters of different ages. As in *Much Ado About Nothing* with its subordinate story line, the entire action in *Twelfth Night,* even with its independent subplot, is unified by a core subject.

A main plot and one related subplot would be quite enough of a challenge for most playwrights, but in *A Midsummer Night's Dream* Shakespeare juggles three story lines, all independent yet related. The one that touches on all aspects of the story involves the quarrel of Oberon and Titania, the King and Queen of Fairies, and the trickery of Puck, Oberon's agent. By means of Puck's intervention, Titania agrees to turn over her Indian page boy to become one of Oberon's followers. But in the course of achieving this, a second, separate plot comes into play that involves the confused affections of two young lovers over which woman they love. Puck is ordered by Oberon to help them in the course of dealing with Titania's obstinacy.

The third line of action dramatizes the story of Bottom, an Athenian workingman, who is victimized by Puck while rehearsing a play in the forest with his friends. Bottom is Puck's means for shaming Titania to yield to Oberon. In this way, Titania, the two young men, and Bottom are all affected by Puck's magic. Its application is the source of comic mischief and confusion—Bottom is transformed into an ass; Titania falls in love with the asinine human; Demetrius and Lysander, who both loved Hermia, now both love Helena. When at last Puck's power is applied correctly for positive means, it leads to a joyous ending for all.

And as if this were not enough, to provide a kind of frame to hold together the multiple characters and events of the drama, Shakespeare opens and closes his play in Athens at the royal court of Theseus and Hippolyta. In the first act they discuss their impending wedding, and in the last we witness their nuptials. In the celebration of their marriage, the two young couples are also joined in matrimony, Bottom and his friends perform a version of the Pyramus and Thisbe legend to provide entertainment, and Oberon, Titania, Puck, and the fairies bless the newlyweds. All aspects of the plot are brought on stage at the end, and we are left with the suggestion that the unreality of what we have just witnessed in the theater might well be thought of as a wondrous dream. In this way our experience is rather like that of Titania and Bottom as well as the four young lovers, who all sense that they have experienced a deep and dream-filled sleep after their night in the forest outside Athens. The many strands of these separate story lines have been interwoven into a beautifully meshed chain of events.[9]

As we have argued, the little drama of Malvolio's gulling by Olivia's servants in *Twelfth Night* or the three self-contained stories that make up much of the action of *A Midsummer Night's Dream* are cleverly managed and integrated with the main plot. But none of these, delightful though they are, involves complex characters in a sequence of events that leads to psychological development. Malvolio exits furious at his tormentors: "I'll be revenged on the whole pack of you" are his last words. His suffering has not brought him any wisdom. He still has not found a sense of humor or gained any greater self-awareness; he proves to be incapable of change. Similarly, in *A Midsummer Night's Dream*, the characters display no capacity for mental or intellectual growth. Their altered affections are involuntary, a consequence of Puck's magic. They are the victims of his actions. The behavior of Titania and the two young men are not determined by complex personal motivation; for the most part, they act involuntarily, compelled by a power they neither understand nor control. The results of all this are comic, for we are watching characters maneuvered into absurd situations beyond their comprehending.

In *King Lear*, a play written some time after these two works, Shakespeare proved his ability to write a fully developed, secondary action with complex, psychologically presented characters. This example is especially interesting, for *King Lear* is the only one of his tragedies with a complete double plot.

Shakespeare reworked an old play, *King Leir*, for much of the main action. He based the secondary plot, the Gloucester story, largely on material from a non-dramatic source, an episode in Sir Philip Sidney's prose romance, the *Arcadia*. By pairing two tales from two very different sources, adjusting what he borrowed to suit his own purposes, and matching events in the main action with those in the secondary plot, Shakespeare created what is for many the most powerful dramatic work in the English language.

Perhaps Shakespeare chose to combine the two independent story lines into one drama because both involve a father who suffers at the hands of one or more of his children but who is loved and cared for by another of them. And the two father figures themselves make an interesting pairing: King Lear is far too absolute, too sure of himself and his judgment. The Earl of Gloucester, on the other hand, is a far weaker man, too gullible and credulous. Each of them could profit by having a little more of what the other one has in excess. Sometimes Shakespeare even points out to us that the two sequences are meant to be held up to one another. Though Lear misunderstands the truth of Gloucester's situation and though the King's remark is full of irony, nevertheless his words point up the paired nature of the two stories: "Gloucester's bastard son was kinder to his father than my daughters got 'tween lawful sheets."

In his dramatizing of the events, Shakespeare has maintained a careful parallel between the growth and development of Lear with that of Gloucester. For example, after both fathers have turned against the child who really loved them and been betrayed by their wicked offspring, their suffering leads them to understand the need for compassion. In their pain, they rightly fear going mad. Lear acknowledges perhaps for the first time that he has "ta'en too little care" to alleviate the misery of the world and senses that his "wits begin to turn." In the same scene, the Earl realizes that he must help the dispossessed old king: "My duty cannot suffer/ T'obey in all your daughters' hard commands." And Gloucester, too, fears that his own personal misfortunes will cause him to lose his mind: "The grief hath crazed my wits."

Although the situation and the sequence of events in both story lines are similar and kept in tandem throughout the play, the two fathers are of such different natures that their response to their experience is hardly the same. In this way, the running comparison implied between the main plot and subplot is now opened up for contrast. Perhaps the single most important distinction to be made between Lear and Gloucester involves their strength of character. "Every inch a king," Lear proclaims to the world despite his wretchedness and misery. He never refuses to face his pain or to fight against his oppressors: "In such a night/ To shut me out! Pour on; I will endure." He understands that life is to be lived, and that whatever happens must be faced with stoicism: "Thou must be patient," he tells Gloucester. Lear is the stuff out of which tragic heroes are made. Such men as this never give up the struggle, even at the very end trying to believe that his beloved daughter might still be alive.

But the Earl is not so stalwart and stubborn a man as Lear. Gloucester cannot overcome the despondency he feels for his mistake in judging Edgar, and the burden of his error and his blindness make life unbearable for him. He attempts suicide. Edgar tries to teach his father something of Lear's stoicism, and Gloucester thinks he has learned the need to "bear/ Affliction till it do cry out itself/ 'Enough, enough, and die." But such a lesson is difficult for so weak a man. He falls into despair a second time when he learns that the army of Lear and Cordelia has lost the battle: "A man may rot even here." And once again it is Edgar who "saved him from despair."

Yet these two fathers die in similar ways. Learning of Edgar's constant love and support, Gloucester's heart "in the conflict . . . / 'Twixt two extremes of passion, joy and grief,/ Burst smilingly." The same is true of Lear who, grieving over Cordelia's body, imagines that her lips begin to move. Like Gloucester, he dies in a moment between joy and grief. The two independent story lines make for fascinating comparisons and contrasts that point up differences among the characters in their personalities, in their morals, and in their affective lives. Indeed, the extremes of joy and misery, cruelty and compassion, anger and remorse demonstrated by those who inhabit the world of *King Lear* are unequaled in dramatic literature for their range, intensity, and theatrical power.[10]

Although the two plots—Lear and his daughters as the main action, Gloucester and his sons as a subordinate story line—are developed separately, at the conclusion of the play Shakespeare has also found ways to integrate them. Lear and Gloucester are reunited a last time at Dover at the end of the fourth act. And in the final moments of the play, both of Lear's older daughters, bitter rivals for the attention of Gloucester's son, Edmund, die in a power struggle for him: "The one the other poisoned for my sake,/ And after slew herself," Edmund tells us. "I was contracted to them both," he confesses as he is dying. Brutality and materialism are characteristic of all three of them, and so appropriately, as he says, "All three/ Now marry in an instant."

King Lear is arguably the finest example in the Shakespeare canon of a dramatic structure that follows two parallel and independent story lines with points of crossing and interconnecting. If one tries to retell the events of this play in the way that Shakespeare has organized them, one will appreciate just how formidable is his achievement. Even when one knows what happens, it becomes a challenge to recapitulate the sequence exactly.

We have considered dramas with single plots, multiple lines of action, and parallel stories, but Shakespeare's ingenuity is hardly exhausted. In some of his plays certain of the incidents in the work do not form a continuous story, for they are completed almost as soon as they are introduced. Although short-lived, such scenes offer examples that relate to an overall unifying, thematic concept and develop our understanding of character. In these works, the action is partially composed of brief, separable, and independent events that make a collective contribution.

In *As You Like It*, the main characters flee from a harsh world, retreating into the pastoral life that exists in the Forest of Arden. Here a number of incidents occur in which those in exile have a series of encounters with those native to the place. No particular story line clearly emerges. From time to time we watch how Rosalind in disguise tests Orlando's love for her, and we witness the amusing confrontations between characters who hold different philosophies of life. Then, at the appropriate moment, all obstacles are surmounted with disarming ease, and the play ends with most of the visitors agreeing to leave the forest in order to return to the everyday world. The action of *As You Like It* is not so much a story as a demonstration of the various ways that people respond to the joys and vicissitudes of life.

A more complex example of this type of dramatic construction can be found in *Henry IV, Part One*. Here a story line is presented in counterpoint with a series of brief, independent, self-contained episodes. Ultimately, the main plot and the separate episodic scenes are woven together at the conclusion.

Two main sets of characters alternately hold the stage in this work: the rebels and their supporters on the one hand and the prince and his supporters on the other. The only sequential story dramatized is the persistent opposition of the two and the determination of the rebels to pursue their dynastic ambitions to a showdown. All their maneuvering will eventually lead to the battlefield at Shrewsbury where the rebel and royalist forces meet.

But in addition to following the political struggle, we are also witnesses to an amusing series of actions involving Hal and his tavern associates. Each of these is so quickly resolved that the individual events in the wastrel life of Hal do not become linked into a continuous story. The adventures of the disguised Prince and Poins robbing their friends and then exposing Falstaff's enormous lies is a delightful episode, but it is over and done with before Act III. The play-acting charade with Hal as his father and Falstaff as Hal is an amusing rehearsal, serving as preparation for that later scene when father and son have their confrontation in earnest. These comic moments contribute more to character development than they do to the story. Personalities and values are being dramatized through these episodes, but no sequential, connected story line emerges that can bind everything together, not at least until rather close to the final resolution of the play.

Before he created *Henry IV, Part One*, Shakespeare had written several chronicle histories, completing his apprenticeship in the art of turning English history into drama. So this first installment on the reign of Henry IV is by any standard of judgment a highly polished work of art. In organizing the story for the stage, Shakespeare made many minor and at least two major alterations to his sources. First, he changed the age of the king's leading opponent. Shakespeare made Henry Percy, or Hotspur as he was called, as youthful as Prince Hal when, in fact, Hotspur was actually older than Hal's father. The second major instance of historical revision was the transformation of the Protestant martyr, Sir John Oldcastle, into the elderly comic figure, Sir John Falstaff. By considering why Shakespeare chose to invent what was never in his sources, we can begin to recognize the unifying principle of this play and its central concerns.

The dramatist's motivation for these changes is fairly certain: they help him shift the focus of the work away from the title character and onto his son. Since Hal will grow up to become one of England's greatest kings, Henry V, in this play Shakespeare considers what aspects of the prince's character and what experiences as a young adult helped him grow into a superb national leader. By making Hotspur Hal's contemporary, the playwright can more easily contrast their behavior. And by turning Oldcastle the martyr into Falstaff the hedonistic, drunken lawbreaker, Shakespeare can dramatize Hal's well-known misspent youth and let Falstaff take the blame.

Since Prince Hal's future development is a central concern of the play, the leading figures around him serve as representative patterns of behavior, and he learns from all of them. Hal considers the lifestyles and values of Hotspur, Falstaff, and his father before reforming himself into the "king of courtesy."[11]

The attempt to overthrow Henry IV is the historical subject matter of the play and forms the major story line. The growth and development of Prince Hal into a potentially great king is what the action dramatizes. But the thematic treatment that forms the basis for organizing the work was settled years earlier in words Shakespeare had written in *Richard II*. In that play, the deposed King Richard, forced to give up his throne, foresees that his enemies will soon quarrel. They will turn on each other, for their new king, Henry IV, can never reward them sufficiently:

> Thou shalt think,
> Though he divide the realm and give thee half,
> It is too little, helping him to all.
> And he shall think that thou, which knowest the way
> To plant unrightful kings, wilt know again,
> Being ne'er so little urged another way,
> To pluck him headlong from the usurped throne.
>
> (V.i)

Thieves will have a falling out, Richard predicts, and his words provide the link that not only connects this earlier work to *Henry IV, Part One*, but also provides the action of the later play with its unifying theme. In effect, Richard is warning Henry and his accomplices—Hotspur's father and uncle—that there is no honor among thieves. And so scenes in which thieves attempt to steal from one another are enacted in both the rebel plot and the Hal–Falstaff episodes. Shakespeare had decided how he would pull the story together long before he actually began writing *Henry IV*.

In the historical episodes we watch how Henry's former associates, who aided him in deposing his predecessor, now form a conspiracy to join forces, start a civil war, and place a member of their own family on the throne. They become, in effect, robbers twice over: having first helped take the crown of England away from Richard and given it to Henry, they now plan to rob Henry, a former member of their band of thieves, and give the crown to another. The dramatist clearly had in mind that when he came to write the sequel to *Richard II* he would dramatize, in the words of Falstaff, "when thieves cannot be true to one another."

As a comic version of what is attempted in the serious political story line, Shakespeare has invented the justly famous Gad's Hill episode. In this action, some travelers are robbed by Falstaff and his associates; then they are set upon and robbed by the disguised Hal and Poins. Yet in this case neither Hal nor Poins actually joined with Falstaff, as he expected them to, and Hal restores the money taken from the travelers with interest added. Shakespeare means us to appreciate how the serious effort of the rebels is reflected in this comic imitation. And just as Falstaff's robbery ends in failure and exposure, so too will the rebels' efforts against Henry IV.

Henry IV, Part One, is a work that is widely admired, for it manages to do many things well: it introduces us in lively and exciting fashion to some of the major historical events and personalities that defined this reign; it develops the character of the future Henry V, preparing the way for the successes that will follow when Hal becomes king; it presents comic moments that by mimicking the serious subject matter broaden our understanding of the issues raised by the action; and it functions both as an independent, freestanding work and as an integrated installment in the cycle of plays on English history.

As we have seen, continually devising new ways in which to shape dramatic structures is a characteristic of Shakespeare's work. So the ability to turn history into art that we find demonstrated in *Henry IV, Part One,* is hardly surprising. Similarly, in at least one of his plays on classical history, Shakespeare also experimented with dramatic structure in a radical manner. In *Antony and Cleopatra,* the playwright needed to find a means of conveying on stage the scope and range of the action, which occurs over a ten-year period and crosses the entire Roman Empire from Egypt to Rome and at points in between. To convey this sense of time and space in a way that adds intensity and excitement to the plot, the action is broken up into a rapid series of scenes, some of them extremely short, set in different countries. Act III of *Antony and Cleopatra*, for example, consists of thirteen scenes and Act IV of fifteen scenes; that is more than twice the number that make up the average act of a Shakespeare play. If *Antony and Cleopatra* extended each of these to the usual length, the audience would be in the theater far too long. But by organizing the plot in rather short, multiple scenes, setting these in varied locations, and using messengers to report the latest news from the outposts of the empire, the playwright contracts the historical events of a decade and enhances the play's sense of epic sweep and drama.

Shakespeare, as we noted earlier, twice proved that he could exercise restraint in his playwriting. In both *The Comedy of Errors* and *The Tempest* he confined his drama to a single story line, and he staged the action in such a way that it transpires in one place and in only a few hours. We learn at the opening of *The Comedy of Errors* that the unfortunate Egeon will be allowed only one day to try to save his life. In the next scene we discover that the time is near noon and that Egeon, unable "to buy out his life, . . . dies ere the weary sun set in the west." As the action progresses, we are kept informed of the time: at the opening of the second act "it is two o'clock"; in the last act "the dial points at five." Shakespeare is careful to point out how the plot is accomplished within the narrow time span allotted.

In *The Tempest*, the time sequence of the events that occur on Prospero's island is also carefully noted. The action begins after two o'clock and reaches its completion at six. Prospero tells Ariel early in the first act that "The time 'tween six and now/ Must by us both be spent most preciously." And in the last act Ariel tells Prospero that the clock is "On the sixth hour, at which time, my lord,/ You said our work should cease." The performance time has come close to matching the timeline of the play itself.

The ways in which Shakespeare organizes the plots of his plays, the kinds of structural designs he invents for dramatizing them, vary widely, but, especially in his mature works, the beauty of his plans lies in their fundamental unity as well as in their ingenuity. He seems to be especially interested in relating main plot to subplot, central action to subordinate incidents, secondary characters and their concerns to the main thrust of the story.

Dreaming and marriage unite the events of *A Midsummer Night's Dream*; misguided wooing joins the main plot and subplot of *Twelfth Night* together in theme; the parallel events of the Lear–Gloucester stories unify *King Lear*. And *Henry IV, Part One,* with its twin sets of robbers, is perhaps the most surprising and delightful example of this genius for finding common thematic ground between the serious and the comic. Finally, in *The Comedy of Errors* and *The Tempest*, the two shortest of his works, Shakespeare demonstrates his skill at compressing plots into a twenty-four-hour time span while still dramatizing a wide range of emotions and a variety of incidents. In every case, he achieves this coherence by organizing his material so that it encourages us to make comparisons or to contrast stories, episodes, scenes, and characters.

3

Managing the Exposition

Shakespeare's bare stage allowed him every possibility; its very emptiness meant that it could become anything he wanted. Crucial information was incorporated into the lines. Whatever the particular historical period or setting, whatever the time lapse between scenes or their location, the dialogue could be counted on to provide whatever knowledge is necessary. Without the bother and specificity of physical scenery and without the need to be accurate in costuming, the action could race along unimpeded by anything but the writer's words. The "bookkeeper"—who we today would call a prompter—stood just offstage, and the dozen or so men and four boys who made up the Shakespearean repertory company could play a range of parts. Any actor could "double," that is, he could appear in as many different roles in a single play as needed. All he requires is time enough to adjust his costume—so the audience could recognize who he is meant to be each time he appears on stage.

These basic conventions of the early modern theater were not regarded as liabilities or limitations. On the contrary, the way this theater functioned encouraged both attentive listening to the playwright's language and imaginative participation. Since the action occurred on a bare stage, the audience had to create its own visual setting. In this playhouse, oral clues were essential to learn the particulars of time and place. Active mental involvement was essential. To enjoy the performance spectators had only to do what Shakespeare asked of them in *Henry V*: "piece out our imperfections with your thoughts."

Telling the audience crucial information directly may be the easiest way for any dramatist to get things started. By using a narrative rather than a dramatic mode, the writer can explain to us what led up to the situation that now is about to unfold on stage. Without such background information we will be confused at the opening of the play. Who are these people?; what is their relationship to each other?; what is the problem confronting them?; how did they get into this predicament?

A surrogate for the playwright—a prologue speaker, or presenter, or chorus—can simply fill us in, and then the dramatic action can really get under way. One of the most successful, long-running dramas of the period, Christopher Marlowe's *Dr. Faustus*, offers a textbook example of how to do this. Marlowe starts his play with one of the actors speaking as a chorus, telling us in a soliloquy of nearly thirty lines that we will be watching the history of Dr. Faustus's life and informing us who he is and what he does. We learn that he was "born of parents base of stock" in Germany, that "to Wittenberg he went," that he is overly proud and ambitious, and that he has just now been captivated by the study of black magic.

Marlowe's Chorus speaker then reappears from time to time throughout the play offering us plot information and describing what would be difficult to dramatize. Before Act III, we learn that Faustus has left the study of astronomy for cosmography; before Act IV we are told that he has returned to Germany where he makes proof of his special powers. And at the conclusion of the play, the Chorus delivers a highly moral, if unsatisfying, epilogue.

These speeches serve to hold the work together with their introduction, progress reports, and summation. Such an essentially narrative method, with the playwright speaking in his own voice, proved not to be a grave liability for the writer, for the play sustained its popularity for a very long time. Although it is not a very exciting or dramatic way to engage an audience while filling in the necessary background information, Marlowe's example would have helped make the use of a chorus a common convention in the theater. But rarely, as we shall see, is any theatrical device used in a simple or conventional way in Shakespeare's dramaturgy.

When the Chorus of *Romeo and Juliet* steps onstage to deliver the prologue to this play, no one would have been surprised by his words:

> Two houses, both alike in dignity,
> In fair Verona, where we lay our scene,
> From ancient grudge break to new mutiny.

These first three lines convey nearly all that is necessary to understand the ensuing action. The place, the families, the long-standing quarrel are all key elements. The short opening speech, a Shakespearean sonnet, ends by cautioning us that to enjoy what follows we must "with patient ears attend." The Chorus makes its second entrance in the play at the opening of Act II when it delivers another sonnet.

But the opening scene actually conveys the facts communicated by the Chorus's first speech. The street brawl between the Capulets and Montagues that breaks out almost the moment the Chorus speaker has left the stage dramatizes what we have already been told. We really learn very little from the Chorus that we are not about to find out immediately. So why does Shakespeare write it? It seems that Shakespeare's Chorus does not really function in the manner of *Dr. Faustus*, offering to tell us essential, undramatized background information.

Though repetition of basic material may well be useful, especially at the opening of a play as the audience is settling down, Shakespeare's speech for the Chorus places heavy stress on the tragic nature of the action that follows. In effect, the prologue warns us that we will witness the path of "star-crossed," "death-marked" young lovers. Only "their death" will bring an end to "their parents' strife." These lines emphasize the unhappy nature of the story.[12]

Shakespeare seems to be preparing his audience for the final outcome, and that may be a sensible warning. After all, a story about two young, sympathetic lovers attempting to overcome parental

opposition—an opposition that is presented as foolish and irrational—is the stuff of comedy. The classic love comedy traditionally
celebrates how youthful lovers succeed in marrying despite their
families' efforts to stop them. The initial situation in Verona seems
ripe for a happy ending, and the jocular bawdiness of such a character as Mercutio encourages the audience to expect that all will conclude with nuptial celebrations and reconciliation. By forewarning
and reminding the audience, the Chorus provides important emotional guidance about genre expectations. But after opening the
second act, the Chorus speaker, the voice of doom, is unnecessary.
The deaths of Mercutio and Tybalt, which occur in the very first
scene of the third act, dramatize Romeo's fate: he is "wedded to
calamity." We now need no reminding that all will end in tears. So
Shakespeare's Chorus functions not for purposes of exposition but
for audience preparation. In fact, Shakespeare seems so secure in
his ability to get the action under way and to keep it moving
that his Chorus figures rarely if ever appear only for the purpose
of exposition.

Henry V offers the most complex example of the role of the chorus
in Shakespearean drama. The Chorus in this play has more lines
than any other choral figure in Shakespeare, and, indeed, the actor
who takes on this part has one of the largest in the play. But his
speeches—a prologue, a soliloquy before the next four acts, and
an epilogue—aim only in part to inform us about place, time, or
background.

In stirring introductions to each of the five acts he reminds us
that we are watching only a poor version of history presented as
scenes staged on an "unworthy scaffold." At every appearance the
Chorus apologizes for the limitations of his medium, a practice
that would seem to be contrary to the best interests of the dramatist, who should rather encourage his audience to forget the shabbi-
ness and artificiality of what they witness.

But by emphasizing that the action is only a pale reflection of
the historical reality, the Chorus can put great stress on the need
for the spectator's willing suspension of disbelief; "let us . . . / On
your imaginary forces work," he pleads. And so the playwright di-

rectly takes on the challenge of staging such events as the battle of Agincourt on an empty platform with hardly more than a dozen actors.

Language, of course, is his greatest asset. To assist the audience in its imaginative participation, Shakespeare uses rhetorical and literary devices in these choral speeches that encourage our active emotional and mental involvement. For example, verbs in the imperative mood occur repeatedly. We are not only urged to form a mental compact with the actors but ordered to do so. At the opening of Act III, the Chorus implores us: "Suppose that you have seen," "Play with your fancies," "Hear the shrill whistle," "do but think," "Grapple your minds," "leave," "see." And these are only a few instances. By his constant use of verbs commanding us to join imaginatively with what is happening onstage, Shakespeare raises the level of our emotional involvement. Indeed, the energy and insistence of the Chorus is so forceful that sometimes he even doubles his commands: "Follow, follow!"; "Work, work"; "Behold . . . But now behold."

Shakespeare's multiple references to sights and sounds as well as his repeated use of gerunds describing action also enhance the audience's sensory response to the play's poetry. The following quotation comes from the first dozen lines spoken by the Chorus at the beginning of the fourth act:

> Now entertain conjecture of a time
> When creeping murmur and the poring dark
> Fills the wide vessel of the universe.
>
> . . . .
> The hum of either army stilly sounds,
> That the fixed sentinels almost receive
> The secret whispers of each other's watch.
>
> . . . .
> Steed threatens steed, in high and boastful
>   neighs
> Piercing the night's dull ear; and from the tents
> The armorers accomplishing [i.e., equipping] the
>   knights
> With busy hammers closing rivets up.

(IV)

These aural references—"murmur," "hum," "whisper"—and gerunds—"creeping," "poring," "piercing," "accomplishing," "closing"—convey a sensory and kinetic power that helps us to feel ourselves present in the scene described. Here Shakespeare's verse encourages us to see the "shipboys climbing" on the "sails,/ Borne with th'invisible and creeping wind," whose strengths "Draw the huge bottoms through the furrowed sea,/ Breasting the lofty surge."

We are swept up by the verbal scene painting of these lines, so vivid and lively, so engaging and exuberant. This Chorus is no mere author surrogate who conveys expositional matter in a straightforward, narrative fashion. This orator, an ardent Englishman and a thoroughgoing chauvinist, adores his country and idolizes the protagonist of the drama, "the mirror of all Christian kings" with a "largess universal like the sun." The Chorus establishes mood, arousing his listeners to share in the excitement, to participate in the action, and at the same time he conveys expositional information, explaining crucial matters of place and time that are not dramatized.

In two other works Shakespeare makes use of an allegorical figure to serve as chorus, presenter, or narrator. In this role the actor has no personality other than that defined by his name, but, of course, that name gives the speaker a more distinctive character than Marlowe's anonymous Chorus in *Dr. Faustus*, for example. *Henry IV, Part Two,* actually opens with the appearance of an actor in a costume, according to the stage directions, "painted full of tongues." He introduces himself to us as Rumor. In the course of explaining how Rumor works and the lies he spreads, his speech also includes the truthful information necessary to understand what will follow:

> I run before King Harry's victory
> Who in a bloody field by Shrewsbury
> Hath beaten down young Hotspur and his troops,
> Quenching the flame of bold rebellion.

(Induction)

Once he has told us what we need to know, the play continues without his reappearance. Although he only spreads "continual slanders" to jump-start the action, Rumor functions as a colorful and efficient means of reminding or informing the audience at the start of *Henry IV, Part Two*, of the state of affairs when *Part One* concluded.

The figure of "Time" in *The Winter's Tale* is the second of Shakespeare's allegorical Chorus roles. Since this play requires a sixteen-year pause before it can move to its resolution, time is a crucial factor in the working out of the plot. Time as an actor makes his single appearance when the first portion of the story has ended, just before Act IV. The long break in the plot sequence announced by Time leaves the consequences of the first three acts unresolved—the insane jealousy of King Leontes, the death of his son and wife, the rejection of his baby daughter Perdita, and even the killing of his agent by a wild bear. Yet all the Chorus tells us in his soliloquy is that now, with the action transferred to Bohemia, we will learn of the young prince Florizel and the abandoned princess Perdita, who have both reached maturity in that far country. He will not spoil the suspense: "let Time's news/ Be known when 'tis brought forth"—we'll know it when we see it. In this play the Chorus has a symbolic function. The passage of Time contains the means to bring forth the revelations, the forgiveness, and the restoration of some part of what was lost. To use Time's own words about the beauty of Perdita, the conclusion is something "equal with wond'ring." Indeed, at the very end of the play, Leontes refers to the "wide gap of time" that has enabled the characters to arrive at their final happiness.

The original source for *The Winter's Tale* had the subtitle, "The Triumph of Time." Perhaps this phrase may have initially suggested to the dramatist that an allegorical figure, no doubt with hourglass in hand, would be an appropriate way of staging the passage of years required by the plot. Yet the ending Shakespeare wrote for his treatment of the story is very different from and far more positive than what he found in his original. The grim suicide that ends Leontes's life in the old prose romance is discarded.

In *The Winter's Tale,* redemption and reconciliation are the dominant themes, and a crucial requirement for these healing processes to take place—the passage of time—is symbolized by Shakespeare's Chorus. In this way the figure of Time onstage serves both as a narrative device—telling us where we are and how many years have gone by—and as the appropriate allegorical embodiment of an element crucial for the resolution.

The Chorus in *Troilus and Cressida* appears only once, as an armed Prologue, to introduce the setting of the play and tells us at what point during the siege of Troy the action will unfold. This minimal exposition hardly requires his more than thirty-line soliloquy. Instead of providing specific background information about the major characters, the Prologue seems rather to establish the setting and mood. We learn, for example, the particular names of all six of the gates of Troy, although these have no role in the drama, and they are never mentioned again. We hear references to many of the sites and locations that evoke the story of the *Aeneid* —"Tenedos," "Dardan plain"—but these, too, prove of no importance to the events that will follow. And since the drama about to begin involves the famous, proud warriors first identified in Homer's epic, the choice of language is inflated and grandiose—"princes orgulous," "warlike fraughtage." This seems to be a prologue, then, that attempts to establish the tone of the work rather than set forth the facts.

But the epic-sounding language of the Prologue, his exaggerated word choice—no doubt meant as the appropriate medium for dramatizing the deeds of godlike heroes—proves seriously inappropriate to introduce the underhanded schemes of the morally bankrupt warriors of this play. Although the Prologue may be presumed to have foreknowledge of what we are about to see, he has seriously misjudged its ethical worth. His elevated attitude fails to recognize the unprincipled nature of what follows, since nothing of any personal or moral dignity will survive the action.

The armed Prologue actually establishes the contrast between what we should expect and what we will actually find. That the epilogue to *Troilus and Cressida* is turned over not to this misguided

Prologue but to the diseased bawd Pandarus reinforces this point; nothing worthy of merit in human endeavor can be found in the world of this play. Clearly, the Chorus of *Troilus and Cressida* helps to set up the central conflict of the drama: the crucial opposition between idealism and realpolitik, between the principles of chivalric honor on the one hand and those of practical self-interest on the other.

In order to avoid the narrative mode that results when a chorus addresses the audience directly, Shakespeare begins *Cymbeline* with a dialogue between two minor, nameless characters who have no individualization and never reappear. Since the situation at the opening is complicated, the playwright uses their initial conversation as an efficient means of passing on the background information. Their talk is really nothing more than a kind of catechism in which the first speaker answers in some detail the questions of the second. The second gentleman, in fact, speaks little more than a series of inquiries: "But what's the matter?"; "And why so?"; "What's his name and birth?"; "Is she sole child to th' King?"; "How long is this ago?" The facts he learns are of so basic a sort that they would hardly be unknown by anyone in Cymbeline's country. So this method is efficient, if rather unsubtle. In effect, the prologue has simply been divided between the questions asked and the answers given. And when enough information has been communicated, the play can begin.

As a more dramatic mode of managing the exposition, a playwright might choose to begin his work with a soliloquy by a principal character. This approach draws an audience into greater involvement because, unlike the narrative of an abstract chorus, it encourages an emotional response to the personality of the soliloquizer. Rather than the kind of straightforward, direct address, which we hear in the prologue to *Romeo and Juliet,* a soliloquy delivers information not only about the initial state of affairs but also about the speaker's response and reaction to them. A perfect example can be found in the soliloquy that opens *Richard III.* With this speech, the playwright memorably conveys expository material, establishes the distinctive nature of the principal figure in the drama, and quickly captures the interest of his audience.

In some forty uninterrupted lines of self-expression, the deformed and humpbacked Richard confides to us how he feels about his place under his brother's rule. His speech falls into three logical sections. First is a series of disdainful comments on the indulgent lifestyle of the present English court, each complaint beginning with the word "now." After establishing that "merry meetings" and "lascivious" ways have corrupted the new royal family, Richard then offers a series of counterstatements explaining how he sees himself in this society where dalliance is all. Each of these oppositional points begins with self-reference: "But I that am . . ."; "I that am rudely stamped . . ."; "I that am curtailed . . ."; "Why I. . . ." The speaker next tells us what his intentions are in this new world where he feels so totally out of place:

> And therefore, since I cannot prove a lover
> To entertain these fair well-spoken days,
> I am determined to prove a villain
> And hate the idle pleasure of these days.
>
> (I.i)

Finally, in the last ten lines of the soliloquy, this malicious and quite arrogantly confident protagonist reveals what plans he has under way to eliminate his brother Clarence, a potential rival for the crown of their sickly brother, Edward IV.

After his soliloquizing, we watch Richard interact with other members of his family and with agents of his brother's court. What we see is a man far more vigorous, quick, intelligent, amusing, and clever than anyone around him. And although he freely admits to us that he intends no good to anyone, that he acts in ways intended only to benefit himself, we find ourselves fascinated by his energy, by his combination of talents, and by his delighted, thoroughgoing dedication to evil.

This opening scene ends with a twenty-line soliloquy in which Richard sums up what we are to appreciate about his special abilities. He confesses that he wants both of his older brothers removed so that they will "leave the world for me to bustle in!" Denying us anyone who can rival his command of the stage until very late in the play, Shakespeare presents Richard as such a dominating and shamelessly beguiling villain that we are fascinated by his high ambitions, by his means and methods.

The necessary expositional material for *Richard III* has been incorporated in the protagonist's self-revelation. Richard tells us what we need to know, then he shows himself in action making good on his self-appraisal, and, finally, he brings this first scene to a close with the confidential admission of his own self-conceit. His two soliloquies frame the central action—his successful deception of Clarence, Brakenbury, and Hastings—so that through this sequence we understand the initial circumstances, and we discover the fascinating nature of the protagonist at the same time.

Rather than the protagonist's soliloquy opening and closing the first scene of the play, Shakespeare has the first scene of *Antony and Cleopatra* open and close with the conversation of minor characters who present a distinct point of view on the action.[13] At the start of the play, Philo tells Demetrius, in a speech which is hardly more than a dozen lines long, to watch the two principals as they now make their entrance on stage, "and you shall see . . . / The triple pillar of the world transformed/ Into a strumpet's fool. Behold and see." Philo's critical judgment of Antony prepares us for the interchange that follows as the Queen of Egypt demonstrates her power over the Roman general, whose devotion to her is without qualification.

After the two lovers have made their exit, Philo and Demetrius, commenting on what we have just witnessed, lament Antony's abandonment of Roman virtues. These men, unhappy friends of Antony, establish for the audience one of the two sets of value systems by which we will ultimately have to judge the action: Roman duty, honor, and state service vs. Egyptian love, pleasure, and self-fulfillment. Yet, neither Philo nor Demetrius reappears after this first scene; they are simply a means to express one possible response to what we shall see and to get the action under way. By starting the play with their comments to each other, Shakespeare avoids the direct address of a choral speech or a soliloquy as well as the heavy-handed dialogue of questions-and-answers we have observed in *Cymbeline*. This tripartite initial scene, similar to what we have described at the opening of *Richard III*, establishes a context for the action to follow and defines a particular point of view toward it.

Some of the most complex works in the Shakespeare canon begin with conversations that draw us into the action. We witness events that are violent, or surprising, or riveting, that not only capture our interest but also arouse our suspense, establishing a distinctively charged world. In the process, some expository material manages to get communicated as well. Scenes such as these determine the tone of a work, defining the atmosphere, or mood, or moral universe in which the drama takes place as well as guiding the audience's response.

The opening scene of *Hamlet* is justifiably admired as among the most successful in all of dramatic literature. The first words spoken are between the departing soldier, who has finished his turn on duty, "sick at heart," and his relief guard. It is a "bitter cold" midnight out on the battlements of the castle. Seven of these initial twenty lines of dialogue are in the interrogative mode—"Who's there?" "Bernardo?" "Who is there?" "Who hath relieved you?" The last of these questions is the most ominous: "What, has this thing appeared again to-night?"

Since the soldiers' guest, Horatio, seems skeptical of what has been reported, Bernardo begins what we quite logically expect will be an explanation. What is it that has appeared; what is the situation unfolding before us? We anticipate that answers will be forthcoming as the exposition begins:

> BERNARDO: Sit down a while
> And let us once again assail your ears,
> That are so fortified against our story,
> What we two nights have seen.
> HORATIO: Well, sit we down,
> And let us hear Bernardo speak of this.

We can relax in our seats, for we are now about to hear a lengthy tale of the events that led up to this moment:

> BERNARDO: Last night of all,
>   When yond same star that's westward from the pole
>   Had made his course t'illume that part of heaven
>   Where now he burns, Marcellus and myself,
>   The bell then beating one . . .
>
>   (I.i)

While speaking these lines the actor playing Marcellus presumably points in the direction where we are to imagine seeing the star "that's westward from the pole." Those onstage with him no doubt look up in that direction as well, and we, watching them, follow their lead. At this moment Shakespeare has written the stage direction: "Enter Ghost." With our attention diverted, the ghost of Hamlet's father makes its unexpected and unnoticed entrance. Marcellus then interrupts Bernardo and shouts suddenly, "Look where it comes again." Even Horatio finds the sight "harrows me with fear and wonder." The ghost refuses to answer its questioners and "stalks away."

After a few lines of comment on what we have just seen, Marcellus asks his friends to "sit down, and tell me" what is happening in Denmark. At this point, Horatio at last delivers some background on the political situation in the country and its opposition to Norwegian ambitions. And just when we think we're now well into the forward movement of the play, the ghost reappears briefly a second time, and again remains silent.

The mood of the work has been thoroughly established, and the brief expository material offered here has been sandwiched between the two separate entrances of the ghost. The action, which began with the arrival of the relief, ends as this group of soldiers disbands, and the blackness of midnight begins to give way to the first light of dawn, in "russet mantel clad." The cold darkness of the initial moments gradually dissolves in the pale light rising over the "eastward hill." Like the temporal progress of the scene, moving out of darkness to distant and faint illumination, we are no longer fully in ignorance, but as yet we understand very little.[14]

Although the opening has a sense of completeness, the atmosphere remains thrilling and strange, filled with uncertainty and doubt. Even those who might be expected to be well informed admit, "I know not," or they reveal their incertitude in offhand phrases: "At least the whisper goes," "I think it be no other," "Some say," "So have I heard." How could we not be curious as we join them in a world so full of hints and suggestions, questions and suspense?

Like *Hamlet, Macbeth* opens with a startling and disturbing action that defines the world of the play. As thunder roars, we are confronted by three witches who appear "so withered and so wild in their attire/ That [they] look not like th'inhabitants o'th'earth." In a very brief scene, of little more than a dozen lines, the three agree to their next reunion on the heath where they will meet with Macbeth. Their presence, their apparent omniscience, their rhyming chant, their description of the time—"foul is fair"—quickly establish the moral universe of the play. What is lost or won, what is fair or foul cannot be clearly discerned in this atmosphere where things are seen only as they "hover through the fog and filthy air." Although they may not be the cause of Macbeth's error in judgment, we understand how in such a world as this, where riddling, bearded old women can look infallibly and ambiguously into the future, a man "full o'the milk of human kindness" can degenerate into a "bloody butcher."

In Shakespeare's late romance, *The Tempest*, the supernatural also has an important role, but in this case its employment leads to a positive conclusion. Although the play's first scene justifies the title, the violence of the opening is not representative of this work. Rather than continuing to follow his usual practice and establish the mood of what will follow, Shakespeare's initial scene here proves to be in sharp contrast with the rest of the play. In these initial moments, the lines need to be shouted, for the actors must be heard over the stage direction: "tempestuous noise of thunder and lightning." On stage we witness a fierce storm at sea and all that it entails—the frenetic movement of the sailors, the rapid entrances and exits of other frantic characters, the sound of "a confused noise within," and finally the terrible cry "we split," dramatically repeated five times. And even as we struggle to understand the players' words over the bustle and sound effects, we will learn little of the exposition in the sixty-odd lines that make up the first scene. In fact, we discover hardly more than a king and prince are aboard the sinking vessel.

Yet the harsh noises offstage and the violence of the opening will soon become modulated into harmonious sounds as the action progresses toward eventual reconciliation and forgiveness. We, too, shall listen to the music that Prince Ferdinand describes as traveling "upon the waters/ Allaying both their fury and my passion/ With its sweet air."

In this first scene, Shakespeare has provided us neither with background information nor with a gauge to the general mood or atmosphere of the play. Rather he has given his work both an exciting start and an initial action that stands in sharp contrast to what follows. The real exposition, delivered in the very next scene, begins when Prospero, in speeches of considerable length, explains to his daughter the painful history of their arrival on the island as well as how and why he created the storm we have just witnessed. As he has done in *Hamlet* and *Macbeth*, Shakespeare seems to prefer to shift the burden of the exposition from the opening of his play to the second scene.

Shakespeare may even occasionally choose to start a play with a scene that establishes mood even at the cost of dramatic action. At times he evidently viewed the need to establish the right worldview as essential for the cohesion of a particular story. *Twelfth Night*, for example, opens not with dialogue but with the sound of sweet and melancholy music. A lovesick Duke, affected and egotistical, mopes about full of self-pity for his unrequited love. He listens to the melody, which he interrupts from time to time, with so fickle and restless a disposition that, as he admits, his spirit of love can reduce whatever is valid and pleasurable "into abatement and low price/ Even in a minute." Then we learn from the reports of Orsino's agents that the Countess Olivia, who has continually refused the Duke's declarations of love, is behaving in as willful a fashion as Orsino. She intends to mourn the loss of her brother by retiring from life for seven years and weep every day. As her uncle remarks, "What a plague means my niece to take the death of her brother thus?" When the Duke hears of her continued rejection, he rushes offstage "to sweet beds of flow'rs," for there, he explains, "love-thoughts lie rich when canopied with bow'rs." Such is the world of *Twelfth Night*.

What willful foolishness! These spoiled aristocrats behave in an irresponsible and unhealthy manner. With the arrival of the hero-ine, Viola, in the very next scene, we soon realize just how self-indulgent they are. Although she shares the same emotions as Or-sino (frustrated love) and Olivia (grief at a brother's loss), Viola's behavior will stand in sharp contrast to theirs. For Viola is ener-getic, vigorous, and positive in her outlook; she demonstrates a de-gree of self-control very different from the pattern of willfulness that prevails even among the servants in Olivia's household. Shake-speare's opening sequence enables us to appreciate his heroine's good sense and strong character more readily after we have wit-nessed the languid boredom that pervades the aristocratic society of Illyria.

So the first scene of the play establishes the background against which Viola's better nature will stand out. And although she ar-rives on the shores of Illyria directly from a shipwreck, Shake-speare begins his play not by dramatizing the excitement of that moment, as in *The Tempest*, but rather by defining the dominant mood of Orsino's country, the setting for the action of *Twelfth Night*.

Shakespeare's works present an exceptional variety of opening scenes because he constantly experiments to determine the advan-tages of starting a play with a new approach. The importance of these first scenes as pointers to what will follow explains why he gave them special consideration: they are keys to engaging the audi-ence, to launching the plot, and to introducing aspects of theme and character. Of course, we can hardly accept as literally true the description of his first editors that his papers had scarcely any evidence of rewriting, but this compliment suggests that a good deal of planning, a firm sense of direction and intention, were well established in the playwright's mind before his hand ever raised the quill to the inkwell to write the first line of dialogue.

4

Structuring and Sequencing the Scenes

To achieve a high level of dramatic unity, Shakespeare has to focus his attention on both the construction and the sequencing of individual scenes, since these are, after all, the basic elements for creating a play. Numerous factors must be considered before a playwright can determine the content and length of individual scenes and the order in which they will occur. For Shakespeare, a scene begins every time an actor or actors enter onto a cleared stage. The process of breaking down the story into its individual episodes and determining their order and length also requires the dramatist to take into account the availability of his players: when performing their roles, which members of the company can act more than one part, and how can these parts be assigned so that an actor never has to appear in more than one role in the same scene.

A new scene often occurs when the action has shifted either in time or place since the actors enter on an empty stage. In *As You Like It*, Shakespeare's refugees announce their arrival in the pastoral world:

> ROSALIND: Well, this is the Forest of Arden.
> TOUCHSTONE: Ay, now I am in Arden, the more fool I.
>   When I was at home, I was in a better place, but
>   travellers must be content.

(II.iv)

When Viola makes her second appearance in *Twelfth Night*, we learn in the very first words of the new scene not only where she is but how much time has passed since we last saw her. She is no longer on the Illyrian seashore, where we left her, but now she is living at Orsino's court, where she has found employment: as one of his attendants says, "If the duke continue these favors towards you . . . you are like to be much advanced. He hath known you but three days and already you are no stranger." If we need to know the where and when of a new scene, we will be informed usually very early in the dialogue. If we are not told, then we need not concern ourselves with such questions.

The shaping of the story line, which naturally determines the disposition of its major scenes, must be arranged to achieve the maximum dramatic effect. In plotting the action of *Hamlet*, for example, Shakespeare spaces out the three major confrontations between the two principal opponents at appropriate intervals. The meetings between Hamlet and his uncle occur at critical moments in the play: immediately after the opening (I.ii)—to establish their mutual distrust; at the turning point (III.ii–iii)—when Hamlet has learned the truth of Claudius's guilt, and Claudius knows this; and at the conclusion of the work (V.ii)—when Hamlet finally kills his uncle. Similarly, Shakespeare spaces out his references to Fortinbras, the Norwegian prince who succeeds to the throne of Denmark at the end of the play. Since Fortinbras has a minor but crucial role in the story, Shakespeare has him discussed briefly in the first two acts. Then the playwright arranges to bring him onstage in Act IV to deliver some eight lines. After this brief introduction, the audience will be able to recognize Fortinbras when he reappears in the very last moments of the play to bring it to a close.

Shakespeare also seems careful to arrange the parts of an individual scene in a highly balanced manner. Act V of *Macbeth* opens with Lady Macbeth's gentlewoman and her doctor discussing her condition. Their conversation, of some fifteen lines, prepares for her appearance. They watch and listen to her for the next fifty lines. After she leaves the stage, the two remain for an additional ten lines to comment on her mental state and the situation in Scotland. In this way the scene has a prologue, a central action, and an epilogue, in which the opening and closing are of about the same length.

Once the overall structure for a play has been worked out and the order of the events fixed, the playwright can actually begin to compose the scene. To do this well the dramatist must take into account that language should reveal not only motives and responses but also something of a particular mind-set and personality, as he does with Lady Macbeth's sleepwalking revelations. Ben Jonson expressed this point in concise fashion: "Speak, that I may know thee."

At the same time that such practical matters demand attention, Shakespeare's interest in unifying his material, in providing a coherent design, leads him to organize scenes so that comparison and contrast are encouraged, and episodes are intentionally paired or placed where their differences and similarities can be immediately perceived.

In *Othello,* the turning point of the action, Act III scene iii, is a fine example of Shakespeare's skill at dramatizing a crucial sequence in a powerful manner.[15] At the start of the scene, the Moor is confident, deeply in love with his new Venetian wife, and certain of her fidelity. As she exits, he remarks:

> Perdition catch my soul.
> But I do love thee! And when I love thee not,
> Chaos is come again.

Iago then begins to ask Othello a series of questions designed to raise doubts in his mind, questions that suggest that Othello may be mistaken in his estimate of Desdemona. In his discussion, Iago quite carefully plants all the seeds that will bring his poisoned fruit to maturity: Desdemona's friendship with the handsome Michael Cassio; the differences in age and race between the newlyweds; the deception she practiced in eloping with the Moor; the reputation for promiscuity and infidelity of Venetian women; and, finally, the torture caused by jealousy. Othello finds he is "not much moved" by these insinuations, but, little more than one hundred lines later, the affirmation of his love is expressed with far less confidence: "I do not think but Desdemona's honest."

In the soliloquy that follows, Othello, brooding over Iago's remarks, begins to convince himself that his wife is indeed untrustworthy. Now, when she reenters, Desdemona tries to cure Othello of the headache he complains of—"I have a pain upon my forehead here"—by binding his brow with her handkerchief. Annoyed with her because of his own unexpressed doubts and fears, he rejects her offer of help—"Let it alone"—and the handkerchief, unnoticed, falls.

A Renaissance audience would have known that Othello's complaint was thought symptomatic of men whose wives were unfaithful: since such husbands were said to sprout horns on their brows, Othello is clearly fearful that he is beginning to show the signs of his wife's infidelity. He will be the butt of lewd jokes and held in contempt by the soldiers he commands, for cuckolds were the subject of ridicule and scorn, belittled as men who could neither satisfy their wives nor keep them honest. The handkerchief, whose assistance Othello has rejected, will come into the hands of Iago, who will make of it the absolute proof of Desdemona's adultery. Shakespeare has placed the loss of the handkerchief, a crucial moment in the development of the plot, at the center of this scene which occurs in the middle of the play.

The second half of this episode then enacts how Iago makes full use of what will become so pivotal in the action. In a brief soliloquy, he decides to plant the handkerchief in Cassio's rooms. Knowing that he has already had some initial success, Iago reasons that with a man of Othello's insecurity:

> Trifles light as air
> Are to the jealous confirmations strong
> As proofs of holy writ.

The Moor returns, distraught, agonized by his doubts and fears, demanding "ocular proof." Leading him on, Iago asserts as conclusive evidence of her infidelity that Desdemona gave Cassio her handkerchief, Othello's first gift to her. Even before he has witnessed the truth of this claim, Othello is ready to believe the worst:

> Look here, Iago:
> All my fond love thus do I blow to heaven.

The scene ends with the horrifying exchange of vows between the two men. Othello gives Iago his absolute trust; Iago responds with the chilling closing line: "I am your own forever."

The action is presented in compelling dramatic fashion, clear, precise, and logical. Shakespeare has arranged matters so that all that happens progresses toward a single pivotal moment, when the loss of the object that can prove Desdemona's innocence and the evidence of Othello's mistaken conviction of her guilt are joined together, and the two are manifested, visually and dramatically, before us. Moreover, through the power of its language and its psychological credibility, the scene is both absolutely persuasive and emotionally disturbing. The sequencing of the action, the pacing of the incidents, the movement of characters on the stage, and the intensity of the emotions are all designed by Shakespeare with complete control over the elements of his art.

But other examples are not difficult to find. Even in a relatively early work like *Richard II* and even when he is not writing the turning point of the action, Shakespeare displays exceptional ability at organizing, sequencing, and pacing individual scenes.

At the opening of Act II, in which John of Gaunt dies, Shakespeare divides the action into three phases: first, Gaunt reminds those around him of the harm that will befall England if the irresponsible and willful young king cannot be controlled; then Richard enters, quarrels with Gaunt, and, continues quarrelling with those remaining after Gaunt is carried offstage to die; finally, after the king's exit, Gaunt's supporters discuss the new state of affairs and announce the imminent return of Gaunt's son, Henry Bolingbroke, from banishment.

In all, this scene totals some three hundred lines. These are apportioned in a balanced manner: Shakespeare writes about seventy lines of dialogue before the King's entrance and the same number after his exit. This leaves the focus of the action on the confrontation between Richard and his opponents, an interchange of one hundred fifty lines, only slightly more than twice as long as what precedes and what follows it. But the King's time on stage is actually bisected by the news of Gaunt's death, occurring at the midway point or seventieth line into the quarrel. Only after counting the lines is the consequence of all this math clear: the entire scene can be divided roughly into four sections of about the same length. The prologue and epilogue are equal, and the main thrust of the scene, divided by Gaunt's death, is twice their length.[16]

In terms of content, the balance is also appropriate. The prologue reminds the audience of Richard's impolitic behavior, preparing the grounds for Gaunt's quarrel when the King arrives. In the main section, after his uncle's death, Richard declares that he is seizing all of Gaunt's estates to finance war in Ireland, and, despite the warnings of his advisors, denies Gaunt's heir his rightful inheritance. This action establishes what will prove to be the grounds for Bolingbroke's rebellion against the king. Then, in the closing section, we learn that Bolingbroke has set sail for England "with three thousand men of war," only waiting for Richard to leave for Ireland. Clearly, Bolingbroke, a clever political opportunist, was preparing to rebel even before he knew of his father's death or of Richard's giving him a strong reason to do so.

Shakespeare's skill at planning, pacing, and sequencing individual scenes is matched by his ability to arrange them so that they can be appreciated in relation to one another. In *Henry IV, Part One*, the important confrontation between the King and Hal over the young man's conduct has first been anticipated by the quasi-comic rehearsal scene, when Hal and Falstaff agree "to practise an answer" and take turns playing the part of the prince and his father. At the opening of Act III, in the episode that immediately precedes the actual father–son interview, Hotspur, who provides contrast to the figure of Hal, is reprimanded by both his brother-in-law and his uncle. Hotspur accepts their criticism—"Well, I am school'd"—but we strongly suspect that his behavior will not change greatly. Hal, on the other hand, who also promises to reform, to "be more myself," will prove that he knows the political value of at least seeming to be generous and gracious. Indeed, one of his critics later admits that the new Hal seems to have "master'd . . . a double spirit/ Of teaching and of learning instantly."

Another notable example of the playwright sequencing and contrasting scenes occurs in *Much Ado About Nothing*. In this instance Shakespeare dramatizes two consecutive examples of trickery through eavesdropping. Both are set in an orchard, and the first, involving the men and Benedict, is followed immediately by the second, involving Beatrice and her female friends. The two being duped are both led to think that they are unobserved eavesdroppers on conversations about them. Benedict hears that Beatrice is desperately in love with him but afraid to admit it, and she learns that he is madly in love with her but afraid of rejection. This bit of deception has been undertaken because those who know them realize that the two will never be reconciled unless they can be made to feel sure they will not be mocked and scorned. Moreover, in each case the deceivers congratulate themselves on what they take to be their certain success. Claudio remarks that if Benedict "do not dote on her upon [hearing] this, I will never trust my expectations," and Ursula feels certain that Beatrice is persuaded of Benedict's love: "We have caught her, madam."

In both these scenes the aim and the method are essentially identical, but Shakespeare has taken great pains to vary the way the two dramatizations are staged. The scene in which Benedict overhears a conversation among three of his friends is some 240 lines long; Beatrice, who also thinks that she is an unobserved listener of the comments about her of two of her friends, has a scene only half as long. Benedict's lines and those he hears are all prose; in the episode involving Beatrice, they are all poetry.

As a consequence, although the action of the two consecutive scenes is similar, both the playing time and the mode of delivery are not. In one instance they are listening to a lively prose discussion in a scene of some length and in the other they are hearing a brief dialogue in blank verse—that is, unrhymed iambic pentameter (a ten-syllable line of alternating unstressed and stressed syllables). Such differences can only be the result of deliberate planning, an attempt by the dramatist to delight his audience with unexpected variety and to demonstrate his skill at controlling plot and organization. Even if playgoers may not be fully aware of the ways these two scenes differ, the variety in these consecutive scenes helps sustain our interest in the action on stage.

Shakespeare also controls or directs his audience's response by the sequencing of the scenes, the order in which they played. *Much Ado About Nothing* offers a good example of the typical Shakespearean approach to dramatizing a comedy. The crisis in this story occurs when Claudio, mistakenly believing Hero has been unfaithful, denounces his fiancée at the altar; she falls into a deathlike swoon, and her accusers are told she has died. But the audience knows otherwise. Even before the debacle at the wedding, they know not only that Claudio and his associates were deceived but also that the local watchmen have learned of the trickery and arrested some of those involved. And they know that Hero is actually alive. So the spectators, in fact, are aware that all the pieces are in place for an eventual happy ending, even if Hero and her friends as well as her mistaken accusers are for the moment ignorant of all of the facts.

Although the members of the audience have more information than anyone on stage, they will remain deeply involved in the unfolding of events. They need never doubt the outcome, but they will remain curious to learn how what they already know will be enacted. From their superior vantage point, godlike, they can look down sympathetically on confusions that are only temporary. This approach to the sequencing of events does not create suspense, uncertainty, or the thrill that comes from the unexpected and the unanticipated. On the contrary, in this situation pleasure is derived rather from the satisfaction of expectations fulfilled. Here, as is most often the case in a play by Shakespeare, things will fall out as the audience had been led to expect they would. When Julius Caesar makes his entrance into the Senate expecting to be crowned King of Rome, he is about the only one in the theater who does not know that he is about to be murdered. What will happen is never in doubt.

Knowing more than those on stage, the spectator can anticipate all
that awaits and smile knowingly as it occurs. Perhaps the work that
best illustrates this principle of Shakespearean drama is *Twelfth
Night*. Naturally, with narrators, soliloquies, and asides all conveying private confidences to the audience, they can be expected to
have a greater awareness of hidden motives and intentions than
most of those actually involved in the action. But in this play some
secrets are kept to the very last. No one on stage in *Twelfth Night*
except Viola herself knows that she is not the boy Caesario until
her final revelation at the conclusion. Only the sea captain,
who appears just once in the second scene of the play, is aware of
her true identity. So Viola has a secret she shares only with the
audience.

But the audience also has information that she does not know:
the spectators find out at the opening of the second act that Viola's
brother, Sebastian, has also survived the shipwreck and is now
"bound to the Count Orsino's court" where his sister has found
employment. All that is needed is to trust to time, a course that
Viola adopted in her very first scene, for these twins eventually to
find each other. And that is a moment the audience can look forward to, its pleasure enhanced by anticipation.

When the twins see each other for the first time since their separation, Shakespeare extends the meeting of sister and brother for
more than twenty-five lines. These two do not rush into each other's arms. As Sebastian looks at Viola dressed in her man's clothing,
he says:

> Do I stand there? I never had a brother
> Nor can there be that deity in my nature
> Of here and everywhere.

> (V.i)

But by a series of questions and cross-examinations they assert
their identities: "My father had a mole upon his brow," she reminds her twin. In the detail and specificity of their answers, with
a positive response following every question—"And so had
mine"—the truth of who they are is ever more firmly established.

Every ounce of pleasure is extracted from this reunion.[17] After all, the audience has waited for four acts for this meeting, a classic recognition scene, and it resolves most of the principal complications of the love tangles. So Shakespeare is not interested in offering realistic drama—the speechlessness that comes with intense emotion, for example—but in presenting a wonderous moment in language and action that raises it to the level of the extraordinary and the unforgettable.

This is an occasion of exquisite happiness. And the mutual love that is now possible for the four principals is all the more wonderful because it is not commonplace in the world of Illyria, where endless frustration and unrequited feelings are all that is left for men such as Malvolio, Sir Andrew Aguecheek, and Antonio. Indeed, Olivia's response to Orsino's suit, "I cannot love him," is more common, even in Illyria as in life, than those rare occasions when hearts and minds are perfectly joined.

Even when aspects of the Shakespearean imagination seem to exceed natural possibilities, they have a rightness that makes them more satisfying than the everyday world. As the father of twins—"Hamnet and Judeth sonne and daughter to William Shakspere" were baptised at Stratford in 1585—the playwright would have understood that only twins of the same gender are identical. But that does not prevent him from making Viola and Sebastian in *Twelfth Night* an identical brother-and-sister pair: "an apple cleft in two is not more twin." But what nature cannot do, great art can. And in so doing, great art is more gratifying, more fulfilling than what life can offer us: "I am Viola."

On the subject of Shakespeare's principle of keeping his audience fully and truthfully informed, one play, *The Winter's Tale*, is the notable exception. Paulina deliberately lies when she tells Leontes that his wife, Hermione, has died: ". . . the queen, the queen,/ The sweet'st dear'st creature's dead." And this falsehood is sustained from this point in the third act until the very last scene of the play. By allowing the lie to remain uncorrected, Shakespeare lets the spectator feel the injustice of the events that have led to the death of an innocent, admirable woman and her son as well as the abandonment of her infant daughter.

But the truth is not totally concealed. Hints are dropped for the attentive. At the opening of the last act, Paulina makes the now-repentant Leontes swear "never to marry but by my free leave." And she says that he shall not have another wife "unless another,/ As like Hermione as is her picture,/ Affront his eyes." Then in the next scene, when we first learn of Paulina's "statue" of Hermione, we hear that it is so like the dead queen "they say one would speak to her and stand in hope of answer." From another reporter we discover that Paulina "hath privately twice or thrice a day, ever since the death of Hermione, visited that removed house" where the statue is kept. As they approach this wonderful object, Paulina warns her company that they should prepare themselves "to see the life as lively mocked as ever/ Still sleep mocked death." And Leontes notices that "Hermione was not so much wrinkled, nothing/ So aged as this" "image" of her when she died sixteen years ago. To this, Paulina merely remarks, "So much the more our carver's excellence."

By this point in the action, we are prepared for the revelation that comes when Paulina orders: "It is required/ You do awake your faith." To her call for music, the stone-still figure moves: "Bequeath to death your numbness, for from him/ Dear life redeems you. You perceive she stirs." This incredible event that takes from death its permanence is performed before our very eyes. If we had not thought Hermione had died, we could not respond so intensely to the miracle of her rebirth, yet we are prepared to witness this moment by the hints and remarks about Paulina's behavior and the "work of art" she protects.

Leontes' sixteen years of atonement and the recovery of his daughter have brought about forgiveness and reconciliation. And like Leontes, who believed Paulina's lie, we have also experienced not only the sense of loss but also the intense happiness of the family reunion—"so like an old tale that the verity of it is in strong suspicion." In this instance, Shakespeare has it both ways: he misleads us in order to engage us thoroughly in the experience, and he prepares us to enter fully in the joyous revelation at the end.

Shakespeare can also manage the sequencing of scenes in such a way that they may comment on each other critically. The import and meaning of what we first see, the interpretation of events presented in one scene, is contradicted or corrected by what occurs in the episode that follows. As a consequence, our understanding of events and ultimately our interpretation of the action must reconcile views which are not in complete agreement, which provide different and even incompatible interpretations of the same event.[18] In this way a simple response to the plot and the characters has been rendered impossible.

The ardent patriotism and righteousness of England in its war with France are exuberantly maintained by the Chorus of *Henry V.* The new, young king seeks assurance from the Church that he may "with right and conscience" (I.ii) claim the throne of France; he reminds his followers that "we are in God's hands" (III.vi); and when the English achieve an amazing victory at Agincourt Henry assumes a proper humility:

> And be it death proclaimèd through our host
> To boast of this, or take that praise from God
> Which is his only.
>
> > (IV.viii)

The country is solidly behind him: "Now all the youth of England are on fire," (II. Chorus) "For who is he that will not follow/ These culled and choice-drawn cavaliers to France?" (III. Chorus)

But among these choice cavaliers are Falstaff's cronies, and these are a sorry lot indeed. The motives of Pistol, Bardolph, and Nym are never noble or selfless. In their case the fire that stirs the "youth of England" is hardly love of country. Pistol leads the threesome away to war with a very different call to arms: "Let us to France, like horse-leeches, my boys,/ To suck, to suck, to suck, the very blood to suck!" The young lad who accompanies them describes their behavior fully: "Three such antics do not amount to a man. . . . They will steal anything, and call it purchase." (III.ii) And the truth of his account is established later in the same act when Bardolph is hanged "for robbing a church."

How are we to understand what we have been shown? How is this sequence of scenes to be reconciled? Henry is surely an attractive figure: eloquent, bold, determined, and capable, "free from vainness and self-glorious pride," as the Chorus tells us at the opening of Act V. The French are arrogant and foolish, but the stalwart English seem to enjoy providential protection.

Yet the blessing of the Church on Henry's plans for war may actually stem from self-interest, for we discover that the clergymen fear the consequences of not supporting the king's claim to the French monarchy. Moreover Henry's true reason for invading France may be to unite England under his new leadership by following his father's advice: "to busy giddy minds with foreign quarrels." The sequence of scenes begins to call into question the professed reasons for his course of action.

A single, absolute motive for any decision may be impossible to determine, of course, for actions are undertaken usually for a variety of reasons, some of them possibly even contradictory. In *Henry V,* the king's awareness of what is in his best interest is so often in the forefront of his mind that one suspects ego and politics rather than altruism or patriotism play a greater role in his decisions. So contrasting behavior is demonstrated in the sequence of contrasting scenes. Henry gives explicit approval of Bardolph's execution not because the theft was impious or sacrilegious but because it will help the English cause:

> we give express charge that in our marches through the country there be nothing compelled from the villages, nothing taken but paid for; none of the French upbraided or abused in disdainful language; for when lenity and cruelty play for a kingdom, the gentler gamester is the soonest winner.
>
> (III.vi)

By dramatizing scenes that illustrate conflicting motives, Shakespeare shows us that his characters have a variety of motives for their behavior. He understands that we are rarely aware of all the reasons why someone acts as he does. Indeed, at times we may not fully appreciate our own motivation.

Another and even more subtle Shakespearean observation about human behavior is that people are capable not only of behaving in contradictory ways but also of sustaining contradictory attitudes. Shakespeare knows that the same set of circumstances will appear very different if we shift our point of view. Angry with Antony, yet as in love with him as ever, Cleopatra compares him to one of those canvases that look entirely different when we shift our perspective: "Though he be painted one way like a Gorgon,/ The other way's a Mars." (II.v) Or as Orsino notes in *Twelfth Night* when he sees the identical twins Viola and Sebastian side by side: "A natural perspective that is and is not." By carefully selecting scenes that show different aspects of the plot and placing these in a sequence so that they naturally reflect on each other, Shakespeare organizes his material in such a way that the richness and complexity of the characters and their actions are fully dramatized.

5

Creating Character

S hakespeare begins with a story and creates characters capable of enacting it, so the challenge of working out the dramatic construction is inseparable from that of inventing those who perform it. What his characters do is who they are; they and the plot are inextricable. Hamlet, Shakespeare's Danish prince, is surely among the most fascinating and complex of all literary creations. How does the playwright construct such a figure out of words on a page and a series of actions? Where does he come from and where does the playwright start?

First, the artist must begin with story. *Hamlet* is a young man who learns of his father's murder, identifies the murderer, and achieves his revenge. But this is a gross simplification of what this work is about or how the tale is dramatized. Although it has only one story line, Shakespeare manages to present us with two other young men, in predicaments similar to those of the hero, whose behavior we witness. Their responses and reactions help us clarify our feelings about what the hero does and how he goes about it. And if this were not enough, the action also involves not only a play-within-the-play, that combines elements from both the murder and the revenge for the murder, but also a recitation about still another young man whose behavior is in response to the death of his father.

Shakespeare helps us begin to understand Hamlet by offering these examples of young men in a similar situation. Like all literary characters, this protagonist cannot be appreciated apart from all the elements of the play in which he appears—language, context, and other characters whose behavior provides a way for us to begin to make judgments. Although aspects of a dramatic work may be separately analyzed, each can be fully understood and appreciated only as a part of the whole entity.

Literary characters also have literary antecedents. Shakespeare's Danish prince has at least one popular precursor: the hero of the revenge tragedy who shares his name. This ancestor, a pre-Hamlet Hamlet, made his first appearance on stage in an earlier work about which little is known. No printed text has been found; all we know of this primitive revenge play, acted perhaps more than ten years before Shakespeare's, is that the hero confronted a pale-faced ghost crying "like an oyster-wife, 'Hamlet, revenge.'"

So Shakespeare had a rough template on which to begin to fashion his protagonist. His audience, too, would have expected a revenge play to include a number of conventional elements. For example, no self-respecting playwright working in this genre could possibly omit a ghost, whether pale-faced or not, who names as his killer a ruthless villain, power-hungry and remorseless. And no self-appointed revenger could live up to his stereotype unless he endured what seemed to him an interminable delay in discovering the guilty parties and effecting his revenge. The severe emotional strain caused by the delay might well explain the occasional fits of madness that afflict the typical hero. At some point in the action, the mysterious hand of providence could also become manifested in the action, but, as we might expect, divine intervention works in a manner beyond our understanding. And, finally, a clear resolution, with the hero achieving his revenge, could be anticipated. The bloodbath that would bring these matters to a conclusion would probably occur during a highly theatrical moment—typically a banquet or a play-within-a-play. Interestingly enough, such an event would have been initiated not by the hero but by the villain.

With all these elements as a part of the usual mix that defines a revenge tragedy, *Hamlet* gives the audience everything it expects to see, and more. In this case, Shakespeare not only adopted every convention of the genre but also incorporated them in new and surprising ways.

Indeed, the work must have been especially fascinating to its first viewers. The ghost of Hamlet's father, for example, is hardly typical of the species that inhabited plays of this kind. This apparition is no fury screaming for vengeance, but a spirit filled with both anger and deep sorrow. In life a man of high principle, he is shocked by the actions of both his brother, Claudius, and his dearly beloved wife: "O Hamlet, what a falling-off was there." Yet the ghost is always solicitous of Gertrude's mental and spiritual state despite her frailty: "But look, amazement on thy mother sits." He is indignant at her remarriage, which occurred within a month of his death, and he is understandably appalled that his own brother "whose natural gifts were poor/ To those of mine," has been able to win her over.

Although unforgiving of his brother—"that incestuous, that adulterate beast"—the ghost orders his son not to "contrive/ Against thy mother aught. Leave her to heaven." Indeed, Gertrude's charms must be considerable, for she rivals the political considerations of the king's murder in Hamlet's thoughts. She remains throughout the play a very major concern of all the principal men in the drama. She has retained the affection of her first husband, and her second husband, by his love for her, is turned into a villain of considerable sympathy:

> She is so conjunctive to my life and soul
> That, as the star moves not but in his sphere,
> I could not but by her.

(IV.vii)

Claudius is, in truth, hardly the callous, power-hungry, devious plotter of the conventional revenge play. He feels deeply remorseful for what he has done: "it hath the primal eldest curse upon't,/ A brother's murder." When he attempts to pray, he has the moral insight to realize that in his spiritual state repentance is merely a hollow gesture. This is an opponent who hardly qualifies as a run-of-the-mill Machiavellian murderer.

And the madness and delay that trouble the usual hero of a revenge tragedy are also made more complex and ambiguous in

Shakespeare's play. After all, Hamlet admits that he is "but mad north-north-west; when the wind is southerly, I know a hawk from a handsaw." When it suits him, Hamlet maintains that his "wit's diseased," but in confidence he warns his associates that he may "put an antic disposition on." He reassures his mother that he can separate reality from fantasy: "it is not madness/ That I have uttered."

If Hamlet's manic behavior is largely feigned, that of Ophelia is not. Her insanity is both real and touching. A young woman with little experience of the world, she mistakenly fears Hamlet no longer loves her. In her judgment this is an irreparable loss, for he is a man, in her words, of "noble mind," "th'observed of all observers." She certainly cannot comprehend how the Prince she adored could kill her father, abandon her, and instantly leave the country. The loss of both father and suitor as well as the absence of her brother, Laertes, leads to her breakdown. In her distraught state, she sings bits of old songs about jilted women and funerals, subjects that offer insight into her mental condition.

Hamlet's delay, too, requires some analysis to distinguish it from what is typical of the genre. The deeply troubled, melancholic prince, alienated from the new court at the opening of the play even before he learns of his father's murder, seems psychologically damaged by his mother's sudden remarriage. His resentment, in fact, is so profound and so intensely concerned with his mother's sexuality that Freudian analysts have offered additional explanations for his conduct.[19] Such a reading also attempts to explain why Gertrude's role in the revenge conflict is so central. To put the Freudian argument most concisely, Hamlet identifies with Claudius, the man who has killed Hamlet's father and married his mother, because that is exactly what every oedipal young man wants to do. But identifying with his uncle makes it impossible for Hamlet to kill him. Hamlet must resolve the contradictory impulses created on the one hand by his psychological identification with his step-father/uncle and on the other hand by his desire to revenge his father's murder. The intensity of his emotions, the anguish and ambivalence of the hero so powerfully expressed in his soliloquies and in his conversations with his mother, lends some rather strong sup-

port to the oedipal reading of the play. Moreover, such an interpretation contributes to the richness of Shakespeare's work; indeed,
Freud admitted that Shakespeare continually astonished him with
his insight into the human mind.

Hamlet's delay is also a factor of the plotting. Once the hero
has verified the ghost's account—"I'll take the ghost's word for a
thousand pound" (III.ii)—he has only one opportunity to kill
Claudius before being sent out of the country. That is the moment
when Claudius is at prayer, and Hamlet decides to wait for a more
fitting occasion to send his uncle on to the next world. In his second attempt on Claudius's life, he stabs through the drapery in his
mother's bedroom at the muffled sound of a man's voice calling for
help. In that situation, the assumption that the voice he heard was
his uncle's is a fairly safe one. Hamlet proves to be mistaken; he
kills Ophelia's father, who was acting as a court spy.

This terrible deed leads to a profound change in Hamlet's attitude toward his situation and his role in the world. With this loss
of his own innocence, he comes to realize that he cannot accept
the responsibility of achieving justice for his father's death without
becoming immersed in a world where injustice thrives: as Shakespeare explains in Sonnet 111, "nature is subdued/ To what it
works in, like the dyer's hand." He needs the help of something
supraterrestrial to rise above the situation in which he finds himself.

In the events that immediately follow on his voyage to England,
Hamlet is brought to a new understanding. He learns to turn to
something greater than himself, to rely on a power beyond his own
control, if he is to succeed. He is saved from Claudius's plot on his
life by fortuitously discovering the king's orders for his execution;
he is able to reseal the king's commands by the accident of the sig-
net ring he wears; he is returned to Denmark because pirates who
unexpectedly board his ship take only him as captive and agree to
redeliver him to his native shores. All of this would be unimagin-
able unless heaven was in control, directing events, or "ordinant,"
to use Hamlet's word. How else could such extraordinary acts have
occurred that bring him back again to face Claudius. With his new
acceptance of his role as the agent of a higher power that will make

occasions right, Hamlet understands that "there is special providence in the fall of a sparrow," that "the readiness is all."

Shakespeare chooses to bring the play to a close through an exhibition fencing match rather than the more typical banquet or play-within-a-play. This results in a far more exciting close since we know how heavily the odds are stacked against Hamlet by the combined efforts of Claudius and Laertes. Yet the match, which leads ultimately to the death of the hero and the conclusion of the play, succeeds in establishing Claudius's guilt in a public manner. After drinking from a goblet of wine, Claudius throws a pearl into the cup ostensibly to raise the stakes of the duel. Gertrude must suspect that he has poisoned the contents, for he repeatedly offers the refreshment to his nephew. To protect him, she drinks—"The queen carouses to thy fortune, Hamlet"—and lives long enough to warn him. Laertes, dying, forgives Hamlet—"Mine and my father's death come not upon thee"—explaining that "the king's to blame."

Hamlet is now no private revenger, guilty of committing an action that reduces him to the same moral level as his uncle, but a public avenger, a restorer of justice in the realm. This is the role in which he wishes to be remembered, and he asks his friend Horatio to live and "report me and my cause aright/ To the unsatisfied."

As a revenge hero who refuses to take the word of a ghost without submitting it to some verification, Hamlet demonstrates his credentials as a Renaissance skeptic and an intellectual:

> The spirit that I have seen
> May be a devil, and the devil hath power
> T'assume a pleasing shape, yea, and perhaps
> Out of my weakness and my melancholy,
> As he is very potent with such spirits,
> Abuses me to damn me.
>
>   (II.ii)

As one concerned with his spiritual condition, who takes seriously the state of his soul in the life to come, Hamlet is unlike the three other examples of young revengers Shakespeare offers in contrast. Laertes, for instance, is one who rejects all moral consideration. In his anger over the death of his father and the insanity of his sister he threatens the king: "I dare damnation." No consideration would cause Laertes to hesitate, to "be revenged/ Most throughly." Indeed, his hatred of Hamlet is so intense that Laertes would not hesitate "to cut his throat i'th'church."

Fortinbras is another prince who attempts to redeem what his father has lost. Recapturing the territories Norway was forced to yield to Denmark would surely improve the young man's standing in his bid for the Norwegian throne, so he has tried out various schemes to test Danish resistance to his incursions. When these are prevented by his uncle, the ruler of the country, Fortinbras receives permission to lead an army across Denmark into Poland. There, according to the text in the second quarto printing, he will fight for a worthless "little patch of ground/ That hath in it no profit but the name." Hamlet, observing this, realizes that "rightly to be great/ Is not to stir without great argument."

The third contrasting revenger is described by a member of the company of actors who visit the Danish court. At Hamlet's request, the lead player recites a speech from an old play in which Aeneas describes the death of Priam and the destruction of Troy. Hamlet asks for this passage in particular for two reasons. In its overly rhetorical style, it describes the savagery of Pyrrhus, the son of Achilles, "horridly tricked/ With blood of fathers, mothers, daughters, sons," who is seeking to avenge his father's death by killing the King of Troy. And it also gives an account of the mourning of Hecuba over the death of her husband, King Priam. So Hamlet can find in it both a possible pattern for himself as revenger and for his mother as a grieving widow.[20]

As it turns out, neither one is a match. Gertrude can hardly be compared to the distraught Hecuba, and the ferocity of Pyrrhus, "roasted in wrath and fire," whom Hamlet finds admirable for his intensity, slaughters every Trojan in sight remorselessly. This is not a model for Hamlet, the prince who learns to accept that "if it be not to come, it will be now; if it be not now, yet it will come."

What is comparable in their behavior is that both Pyrrhus and Hamlet are caught in a similar gesture. As Pyrrhus stands over the old fallen king, his sword "which was declining on the milky head/

Of reverend Priam, seemed 'i'th'air to stick." This frozen action foreshadows the moment when Hamlet stands hidden behind his uncle, who is kneeling in prayer. With his sword poised to strike the king, Hamlet pauses: the realization "now might I do it pat" is held in check by the thought, this "would be scanned." Unlike the "hellish Pyrrhus," Hamlet determines to have revenge at a more appropriate time. Although they are similar in this gesture, Pyrrhus and Hamlet are not alike.

Shakespeare's hero is made distinctive not merely by the individualistic way he meets the requirements of the hero in a revenge drama. Well aware of "the heartache, and the thousand natural shocks/ That flesh is heir to," Hamlet has the sensitivity to appreciate the uniquely human, making him an extraordinary dramatic creation. He knows all the "forms, moods, shapes of grief." He appreciates the need for compassion:

> use every man after his desert, and who shall scape whipping? Use them after your own honor and dignity. The less they deserve, the more merit is in your bounty.
>
> (II.ii)

He understands that all living things should keep in mind "to what base uses we may return."

The last, and perhaps the most important quality in Hamlet, is his enormous capacity for love. He treasures the love of true friends such as Horatio; his school fellows, Rosencrantz and Guildenstern, attest to his capacity for friendship. Hamlet reinstates himself in his mother's love: "when you are desirous to be blest,/ I'll blessing beg of you," and, he reminds Laertes: "I loved you ever."

Finally, he announces the true extent of his love for Ophelia: "Forty thousand brothers/ Could not with all their quantity of love/ Make up my sum." His earlier rejection of her, denying his love and urging her to enter a nunnery, can only be explained as his effort to remove her from the surrounding corruption and to free him to address the cause of restoring justice for the murder of his father. After he heard the ghost's account and swore to take revenge, Hamlet entered Ophelia's chamber as she is sewing. From her description of his behavior it is clear that Hamlet's visit was a kind of farewell: he realized that Ophelia was incapable of aiding him nor would he have been reasonable to burden her with the knowledge of what the ghost has told him. He studied her face carefully, raised a piteous sigh, and let her go "with his head over his shoulders turned" so that his eyes continue their gaze on her. Hamlet's love, it seems, is also capable of self-sacrifice, as all true love must be.

Shakespeare has revealed the mind of the hero in depth by dramatizing the way he responds to an exceptional range of circumstances that call forth an enormous variety of emotions. His words not only express his thoughts but also convey his feelings through imagery that communicates both their passion and intensity. For Hamlet is a tragic hero in the classical tradition: he grows in wisdom through his suffering, and Shakespeare presents this growth on stage in ways that are unexpected and startling. He transforms old conventions in order to show the development of the hero from the idealism that characterizes youth to the mature understanding that comes only with experience. No wonder this is the longest play in the canon; its length is a consequence of its achievement, for no shorter work could accomplish so much.

In the case of *Hamlet*, it was observed that literary characters have literary antecedents. But it is equally worth noting that historical characters in Shakespeare's plays can also have literary antecedents. Indeed, in some cases, they may even have fictional names. It seems that Shakespeare originally used the actual names of such historical figures as Sir John Oldcastle and some of his associates for characters who appear in *Henry IV, Part One*. Later, however, the dramatist rechristened them Falstaff, Bardolph, and Peto. The change was probably brought about largely through the political influence of Oldcastle's powerful Elizabethan descendents, who could hardly have approved of their revered ancestor being presented as a fat buffoon.

But what's in a name? Shakespeare's stage character is not simply a renamed Oldcastle. Sir John Falstaff's literary ancestry can be traced back to several distinct character types that have been blended smoothly together. A part of his ancient family tree flourished in Roman comedy, where some of his ancestors will be found among the braggart soldiers and parasites of Plautus and Terence. Falstaff's hilarious and fraudulent account of how, even when greatly outnumbered, he fought brilliantly—"If there were not two or three and fifty upon poor old Jack"—is a tale that could be expected from any of the boasting officers in Plautine drama. And his outrageous claim that he killed Hotspur is in the same vein, equally bold and equally untrue. Yet he impudently demands, "I look to be either earl or duke, I can assure you."

Shakespeare has also clearly established Falstaff's inheritance from the stereotyped figure of the glutton or freeloader, the parasite who frequently appears in the Latin comedies studied when the playwright was a schoolboy.[21] Indeed, he could have met such a character in Plautus's *Menaechimi*, the play that provided some of the basic material for Shakespeare's very early work, *The Comedy of Errors*. Falstaff's girth, "this huge hill of flesh," is not the only evidence of his love of food. As an indication of his great enjoyment of the table, Falstaff takes as an extreme position the vow: "I'll starve ere I'll rob a foot further"—he would as soon give up stealing as food. Indeed that is true, for Falstaff cannot imagine living without indulging in two of his favorite activities, eating and thieving. His tavern bill includes among other items a charge for two gallons of sack, his favorite wine, with additional "anchovies and sack after supper."

Not all of Falstaff's inheritance is of Roman origin, however. Some of his traits are of native ancestry. Prince Hal is especially aware of these more English qualities in Falstaff's nature when he calls his white-bearded friend a "Vice," and a "misleader of youth." These are, in fact, interesting criminal strains to detect in Falstaff's genetic makeup.

The "Vice" figure is a conventional character in medieval English morality plays.[22] In such works, allegorical characters such as Mankind or Everyman fall prey to the wiles of the Vice, yet ultimately he is defeated and humanity saved. This abstraction personifies all of the seven deadly sins. A devil surrogate, such an embodiment of evil, is a useful stage presence since he needs no motivation for his wickedness: he is evil by definition. He exists to take delight in leading mankind astray, and he uses every temptation to do this. His clever buffoonery and outrageous behavior would have made him both attractive and dangerous, leading his victims on with pleasure and laughter into the paths of damnation.

In addition, in fashioning the relationship between Falstaff and Hal, Shakespeare seems to have in mind another genre of earlier English drama, those based on Bible stories or episodes. In this case, he seems to be thinking of plays based on the prodigal son story, that parable of youth misled by temptation into riotous living, of wickedness corrupting innocence, of repentance and reformation, and finally of forgiveness by a father who kills the fatted calf in celebration.[23] This story is what Hal refers to when he sees his friend as "that villainous abominable misleader of youth, Falstaff, that old white-bearded Satan." Hal knows that his repentance is close at hand. He promises his father: "I shall hereafter, my thrice-gracious lord,/ Be more myself." And with this promise he understands what he must do with Falstaff:

> . . . banish not him thy Harry's company.
> Banish plump Jack, and banish all the world.
> Prince: I do, I will.
>
> (II.iv)

And, indeed, in *Henry IV, Part Two*, once he is crowned king of England, Hal is true to his word. He turns Falstaff aside in that unforgettable rejection, "I know thee not, old man."

Elements of the braggart soldier, the parasite, the Vice, and the "misleader of youth"—these are almost all the ingredients that went into the composition of Falstaff. But the recipe still needs at least one more item: the character of the clown.[24] And in his kind of jesting, Falstaff, with his appreciation of expediency, is more a bitter fool than a sweet one, to use the terminology of King Lear's Fool. Falstaff's way with words is dazzling, for he can redefine, pun, lie, and invent his way into or out of any situation to his own advantage. He is never merely the butt of laughter. Since he has the ability to see both himself and the rest of humanity with some objectivity, Falstaff understands that he is "not only witty in my-self, but the cause that wit is in other men." His inventiveness and zest for life have made him an audience favorite, and, although his death is described in *Henry V,* Shakespeare revived him for a last appearance in *The Merry Wives of Windsor.* That play, so the legend goes, was designed to please Queen Elizabeth, who asked to see Falstaff in love.

Falstaff's incisive cleverness can point up the hypocrisy of thieves who have turned on one another. He reminds Hal, for example, that robbery should be an essential quality in his nature: "thou cam'st not of the blood royal if thou darest not stand for ten shillings." He views the world with no illusions: he can clearly see "the cankers of a calm world and a long peace." He understands that in rather fundamental ways self-interest and self-advantage are for most men stronger motives for action than the humanitarian values they claim to endorse. When Hal says, "I did never see such pitiful rascals" as Falstaff's troops, Falstaff calmly remarks that "they'll fill a pit as well as better. Tush, man, mortal men, mortal men."

Despite his warmth and humor, Falstaff has a cold, terrifying dispassionate nature that allows him to act in ways that deny any social contract or moral obligation. This is "a bitter fool," indeed. His humor is often his means to disguise the fact that his behavior undercuts any belief in a greater good, in a realization that society can exist only through each individual's acceptance of a binding legal code. He freely admits: "Now I live out of all order, out of all compass." Falstaff is an attractive danger: he embodies absolute freedom, and he disregards the unavoidable anarchy that would be the consequence.

Why would Shakespeare design such a character and give him such a major place in a history play? The historical and literary precedents, which established that Prince Hal's chum was a rascal who encouraged the future Henry V in sowing his wild oats, were hardly so compelling that Shakespeare needed to create exactly the figure who became Falstaff or write so important a role for him that he appears in both Parts I and II. He is far more than the scape-goat for Hal's truancy. Shakespeare has fashioned his version of the prince's friend in such a way that Falstaff embodies a distinct point of view, different from that presented by anyone else. His values, his goals, his ambitions are set up in opposition to those of the two other characters, Hotspur and Hal's father, who also serve as spokesmen with their own definitions of what makes the good life. The three philosophies they live by are then dramatized as possible career options for Hal.

With each representative offering a different notion of what constitutes the highest and noblest of life's achievements, the play then focuses on Prince Hal who is at the threshold of maturity, at the moment when he must decide what he will do with his life and the advantages he has been given. Shakespeare has structured the play in such a way that, although it carries his father's name, Hal is actually its central character. And since Prince Hal will grow up to prove one of England's finest rulers, the work takes up the fascinating question of how he managed it.

In essence, then, Falstaff can only be fully appreciated by analyzing him in relation to Hotspur and Bolingbroke, Hal's father. And each of these serves as a possible role model for the prince.

Henry Percy, known as Hotspur, is the rebellious son of a rebellious father. Feeling slighted by the man they helped put on the throne, Henry Percy, with his father and uncle, is eager to unseat Bolingbroke and supplant him with a closer relative. As his nickname suggests, Hotspur is all impatience and hot temper, as attracted by the call to action as Falstaff is to sloth. Movement, busyness, deeds of great daring occupy his thoughts: "imagination of some great exploit/ Drives him beyond the bounds of patience." He would leap to the moon or "dive into the bottom of the deep" "to pluck bright honor."

All of this energy is fueled by Hotspur's obsessive preoccupation with honor, a value he defines largely in terms of victory over his opponents. His boldness and daring make him an attractive figure in the devious world of politics and corruption that Falstaff so pointedly reveals. But Falstaff understands that honor is an ideal reflecting a specific point of view. What is an honorable undertaking in the eyes of some is treason in the opinion of others. The honor Hotspur is fighting for, after all, cannot be considered apart from the material advantages that will come with his successful attainment of it. And in any case, it is, as Falstaff knows, a mere word: "What is that honour. Air. A trim reckoning! Who hath it? He that died a Wednesday." In the end, Falstaff trudges offstage bearing Hotspur's corpse on his back.

Falstaff may be a fool, but Hotspur can be rather foolish. Hotspur's hyper-energetic nature compels him into unreasonable and impractical actions. According to his lights, honor comes when you show the boldness to fight even when the odds are against you. That being the case, it is desirable to go into battle when you are outnumbered. And following this reasoning, the more you are outnumbered the greater is your honor in fighting. Although the logic here might be impeccable, the goal is misguided. Given a choice, one does not enter a battle one cannot win.

Hotspur, however, takes particular pleasure in the fact that some of his allies cannot meet him to swell his numbers. When he learns that his father and their Welsh supporters will be unable to join them by the appointed day, Hotspur insists on challenging Bolingbroke anyway: for to his mind, a willingness to fight under such conditions "lends a lustre and more great opinion,/ A larger dare to our great enterprise."

Such idealism and commitment are attractive in one so young as Hotspur, but his bluntness, his temper, and his refusal to heed older and wiser heads make Hotspur an unsuitable role model for Hal. Hotspur insists on fighting, even overruling the advice of the three more experienced leaders with him: "The number of the king exceedth ours./ For God's sake, cousin, stay till all come in." The consequences are what any reasonable person would predict.

Yet Hotspur makes an important contribution to the drama. His youth and idealism provide a sharp contrast with Falstaff's hedonism and cynicism as well as with Hal's irresponsible behavior. Hotspur is more direct and honest, more committed to principle than anyone else in the play. Hal at least appreciates his virtues and acknowledges them in his public tribute:

> I do not think a braver gentleman,
> More active-valiant or more valiant-young

> More daring or more bold, is now alive
> To grace this latter age with noble deeds.

(V.i)

Hal had promised his father that on the battlefield he would confront Hotspur and "exchange/ His glorious deeds for my indignities." And as the hero of the play, Hal does emerge victorious in their encounter at Shrewsbury. The prince does learn from the youngest and most forceful of the rebels something about the importance of dedication to an ideal that raises existence beyond the Falstaffian pleasure principle. By the end of the play, Hal pays tribute to Hotspur's "great heart."

Yet perhaps the most important influence on Hal's development is the example set by his father. Bolingbroke is a consummate politician. He well understands the art of gaining and holding power, of manipulating a public image, of the limits of honesty, and the uses of deception. He succeeded in seizing the throne of Richard II little by little, correcting abuses, rewarding supporters, making promises. And when he grew so strong that no one dared oppose him, Bolingbroke took the crown itself. As Hotspur can attest, "well we know the king/ Knows at what time to promise, when to pay."

Of course such a clever temporizer and politician as Bolingbroke would find his son's behavior troubling. Unlike Hotspur who "leads ancient lords and reverend bishops on/ To bloody battles and to bruising arms," Hal shows no interest in defending Bolingbroke's reign against its enemies. In fact, Hal seems a surrogate for Richard II, who "mingled his royalty with cap'ring fools." And this conduct is especially distressing to Bolingbroke, for the secret of his success with the public was to be so "seldom seen" that he was rather "wond'red at." In his rare and well-timed appearances, he seemed a warm and considerate friend of the common man, but what they saw was deceptive. Bolingbroke admits that he:

> stole all courtesy from heaven,
> And dressed myself in such humility
> That I did pluck allegiance from men's hearts.

(III.ii)

The ambitious Bolingbroke knows how to play the game of dissembling to his advantage. He has sent out onto the battlefield men in armor who bear the royal ensign: "the king hath many marching in his coats." Bolingbroke is protected by the number of doubles who impersonate him. So dressed, and with their helmets closed so that their faces are hidden, such men as Sir Walter Blunt, for example, can be mistaken for their ruler. When Hotspur identifies the dead man "semblably furnished like the king himself," as Sir Walter, what can a determined rebel like the Earl of Douglas do but vow to continue the hunt?

> Now, by my sword, I will kill all his coats.
> I'll murder all his wardrobe, piece by piece,
> Until I meet the king.
>
> (V.iii)

Such a ploy could hardly meet Hotspur's definition of honor, but Bolingbroke well understands that in practical terms for him victory and survival are inseparable.

Ultimately, Hal does indeed save his father on the battlefield and defeat Hotspur; his military prowess, an important asset for a medieval ruler, is convincingly established. But more important is that Hal proves that he has truly understood his father's principles, and, perhaps, he even goes them one better. Hal demonstrates that he, too, can practice the fine art of political deception. In his very first soliloquy the young prince has warned us that he will "falsify men's hopes" in order to make himself ultimately appear "more goodly and attract more eyes/ Than that which hath no foil to set it off." He is clearly his father's son from the very start. And in the last act of the play he again demonstrates his skill as a manipulator of public sympathy.

Before the assembled armies about to go into battle, Hal challenges Hotspur, offering to "try fortune with him in a single fight" in order "to save the blood on either side." Both rebel and royalist soldiers, no doubt, would approve Hal's proposal for sparing so many lives, especially when the prince so graciously acknowledges that he has been "a truant to chivalry" while Hotspur has no equal:

"I do not think a braver gentleman . . . is now alive." Yet few who hear him understand that this is actually a hollow gesture, for Hal surely knows Bolingbroke is not such a gambler as to risk his kingdom on a fight between his wastrel son and Hotspur.

Hal must realize his father would never allow such a duel, and indeed the king smoothly brushes the offer aside. The noble-sounding proposal has highly positive effects: it wins for Hal the support of soldiers on both sides, yet it holds no real danger for him. Moreover, by this bit of false bravado the son demonstrates that his skill in the art of Machiavellian practices can rival his father's.

In the course of the action, Hal acquires something of Falstaff's zest for life, of Hotspur's sense of commitment, and of his father's political wiliness. In addition to these traits, Hal exhibits a personal warmth and a generosity of spirit that all of them lack. He alone has "sounded the very bass-string of humility"; he has become a "sworn brother" and drinking buddy to the tavern waiters who dub him "the king of courtesy." He can win them over, gaining their approval by his ingratiating manners. The consequences of his indulging in low life are not entirely frivolous for a future ruler: they "tell me flatly I am no proud Jack like Falstaff, but . . . when I am king of England I shall command all the good lads in East-cheap." By the end of the play, Hal's potential as an outstanding monarch is fully established.[25]

Henry IV, Part One, is understandably the most popular, the most frequently performed and studied, of all Shakespeare's English history plays. It covers the historical ground of this period by dramatizing the rebellions that plagued the country under this king. More importantly, it establishes the character of the future Henry V, who grows in humanity and wisdom by the example of those around him. Both the comic and political story lines are tightly unified, and two of the principal characters are particularly memorable. Falstaff is a creation universally admired, and Hotspur is "a part to tear a cat in, to make all split," to use Bottom's description for a juicy role. High emotions, high stakes, and high jinks are the ideal combination for pleasing an audience, and in this work Shakespeare displays a kind of godlike mastery over his medium.

Conventional character types are especially useful to playwrights, for dramatists work under time constraints that do not affect novelists. Since a conventional character—the braggart soldier or the Vice—has attributes that are instantly recognized by an audience, his thoughts and motives, his actions and responses are immediately understandable. This allows a writer to pay less attention to developing character and more to establishing the story line and moving the action toward conflicts that will rapidly engage the spectator. Building characters on stereotypes is a common practice for all dramatists in Shakespeare's day. Occasionally, however, Shakespeare surprises his audience. A figure that at first appears to belong to a well-established type proves on better acquaintance to be not at all what one expected.

A particularly interesting example is the protagonist of *Othello*. The Moor is a greatly respected general, the leader of the Venetian forces, a man who has a high degree of self-confidence and self-esteem based on his lineage and his experience. Surrounded by opponents with drawn weapons, Othello coolly remarks, "Keep up your bright swords, for the dew will rust them." He claims that his was a distinguished family—"I fetch my life and being/ From men of royal siege"—and that he has been fighting "in the tented fields" since he was seven. For him, a black African among Northern Italians, life among the highly cultured and sophisticated Venetians is alien. Their behavior and customs are especially unfamiliar, for Othello admits that he has little acquaintance with life anywhere off the battlefield: "little of this great world can I speak/ More than pertains to feats of broil and battle."

With this as his history, Othello faces a difficult future as the new husband of a much younger Venetian woman. Moreover, as every Renaissance Englishman knew, the women of Venice were thought to be the most refined and subtle in matters of the heart. Love and lovemaking were considered a Venetian specialty; courtesans in that city were both more numerous and more famous than elsewhere in Europe. Iago's slander about Venetian mores, intended to raise Othello's doubts about his bride's faithfulness, was, in fact, held to be true by most of Europe:

> I know our country disposition well:
> In Venice they do let God see the pranks
> They dare not show their husbands; their
>   best conscience
> Is not to leav't undone, but keep't unknown.
>
> (III.iii)

That Othello's new wife would marry him, eloping without parental consent and rejecting the young men her father proposed, "the wealthy curlèd darlings of our nation," suggests that Desdemona could indeed be "gross in sense." It is, in any case, shockingly unconventional behavior. Even the Duke, who tries to reconcile Desdemona's father with his daughter's new husband, compliments Othello with a pun that suggests the Moor, though praiseworthy, is still less than the equal of a Venetian citizen:

> Noble signior,
> If virtue no delighted beauty lack,
> Your son-in-law is far more fair than black.
>
> (I.iii)

Xenophobia, miscegenation, and racism lie veiled behind the thinking of most of these Europeans. Even Desdemona's maid, Emilia, shares in this negative response to Othello's race, remarking that her mistress proved "too fond of her most filthy bargain." With these views so widespread, so commonly felt, Iago's cynical and self-serving comments on Desdemona's character seem entirely persuasive to the foolish Roderigo: "It cannot be that Desdemona should long continue her love to the Moor. . . . She must change for youth: when she is sated with his body, she will find the error of her choice."

What Shakespeare has put on stage, then, is a classic formula for cuckoldry: the older husband; his young and headstrong wife; and her attractive, cultured admirer, Cassio, the Florentine, who is the husband's close friend. This is a combination ripe for a story of seduction, adultery, and its consequences.

Yet these three characters do not follow the patterns common to their stereotypes. They are distinctive, unique. Desdemona is devoted:

> My heart's subdued
> Even to the very quality of my lord.
> I saw Othello's visage in his mind,
> And to his honors and his valiant parts
> Did I my soul and fortunes consecrate.
>
> (I.iii)

In her eyes, even "his checks, his frowns . . . have grace and favor in them."

Cassio, too, proves an honest friend. Although Othello plotted for his death, Cassio, wounded, honestly tells him: "Dear general, I never gave you cause." And at that point in the drama, the Moor knows to his sorrow that this statement is true.

Only one character in this work behaves according to type, and that is Iago. Shakespeare introduces him at the very opening of the play, where he reveals his intense loathing of Othello, and in the last scene of Act I he once more reminds us of his deep-seated feelings: "I have told thee often, and I retell thee again and again, I hate the Moor. My cause is hearted." What is especially noticeable about Iago is the number of reasons he offers for detesting Othello and Cassio: he blames them for his lack of promotion; he fears both men have committed adultery with his wife; he resents Cassio, who "hath a daily beauty in his life/ That makes me ugly."

But all of Iago's motives are suspect. For one thing, there are simply too many. He offers such a variety of explanations for wanting to harm Othello, Desdemona, and Cassio that these seem to be simply excuses or alibis. Moreover, these "reasons" never have any corroborating evidence. For example, neither Othello nor Cassio ever shows the least sign of inappropriate familiarity with Iago's wife. And Desdemona's purity and innocence seem in themselves sufficient to arouse his hostility: "So will I turn her virtue into pitch/ And out of her own goodness make the net/ That shall enmesh them all."

In modern clinical jargon, Iago is a psychopathic personality, that is, one with an asocial, perverse, irrational, and criminal mind. The poet Samuel Taylor Coleridge coined the phrase *motiveless malignity*, giving Iago's disorder a more literary and less medical label.[26] Lacking such terminology, the Renaissance stage thought of such characters as derivations of the Vice figure, those allegorical embodiments of pure, unmotivated evil. And in this case, Iago's cruelty, the sadistic pleasure he takes in causing suffering, is an integral part of what can properly belong to a Vice. Othello finally understands his true nature when he expects to find Satan's cloven hoof on this fiend: "I look down towards his feet—but that's a fable." After he has been arrested, the Moor asks: "demand that demi-devil/ Why he hath thus ensnared my soul and body." Since Shakespeare would not have found it difficult to provide Iago with a convincing motive, the playwright must have decided it was better not to give him one. (In the source, the Iago character is angered when Desdemona spurns his advances.) Without a plausible explanation, Iago's behavior is even more intriguing and chilling; his actions are more horrifying precisely because they are incomprehensible.

That Desdemona has a direct, honest, trusting nature makes her easy prey for such a clever and devious schemer as Iago. His second victim, Cassio, ashamed and remorseful for his drunken brawling, can be easily taken in by Iago's basically sound advice. But corrupting the noble, brave, and cool-headed Othello would challenge anyone.

Yet Shakespeare has laid the groundwork for Iago's approach in the way the tragic hero is presented to us. When Desdemona heard Othello's history, he tells the Venetian Senate, "she loved me for the dangers I had passed,/ And I loved her that she did pity them." Othello's life has been filled not with great victories and remarkable conquests but rather:

> most disastrous chances,
> Of moving accidents by flood and field;

> Of hairbreadth scapes i'th' imminent deadly
>   breach;
> Of being taken by the insolent foe
> And sold to slavery.
>
> (I.iii)

This is not a stirring saga of brilliant triumphs. It is the story of a man whose whole life has been filled with hardship and pain, of survival barely snatched from the jaws of defeat and death.[27] As Othello reminds his audience, "The tyrant custom, most grave Senators,/ Hath made the flinty and steel couch of war/ My thrice-driven bed of down." He is used to suffering, finding himself so often in challenging and difficult situations that he has come to recognize an easy familiarity with hardship, "a natural and prompt alacrity/ . . . in hardness."

Indeed, Othello's excited reunion with Desdemona in Cyprus at the opening of Act II seems to him so unusual, so exceptional, that he greets her with an extraordinary welcome:

> It gives me wonder great as my content
> To see you here before me. O my soul's joy!
> . . . .
>   If it were now to die,
> 'Twere now to be most happy; for I fear
> My soul hath her content so absolute
> That not another comfort like to this
> Succeeds in unknown fate.
>
> (II.i)

The speaker has this instant been reunited with the woman he has only just married; actually, their marriage has not yet been consummated. Othello should be looking forward to a happy future with Desdemona. A well-adjusted bridegroom would hardly wish for death at this moment because he feared he would never again be so happy. But for this soldier, happiness has been always rare and transient. Experience has scarred Othello; he can only ever expect the worst. He is such a pessimist that his love for Desdemona and her devotion to him make him uneasy: "I cannot speak enough of this content;/ It stops me here; it is too much of joy."

Othello's devotion to his wife and her love for him are to an exceptional degree the only value in life: "where I have garnered up my heart,/ Where either I must live or bear no life." But staking so much on this relationship makes it dangerous for those involved if it should come under question: "when I love thee not,/ Chaos is come again." And if one of the two principals is an insecure pessimist, a man who has never trusted in the kindness of his fate, a man who believes he was not cut out for happiness, a man who has only experienced repeated instances of disappointment and pain, then Iago's scheming has found fertile ground. Othello is an easy mark.

Shakespeare has fashioned a remarkably subtle hero in *Othello.* Despite his physical strength, the Moor is defenseless against Iago, against his insinuations, his superior knowledge of the customs of the country, and his "proof ocular," the stolen handkerchief. Othello is so psychologically vulnerable that when he is joined by such characters as Iago and Desdemona, the terrible consequences seem inevitable. Unlike all of Shakespeare's other tragedies, this one, involving only three principal actors in a brief, domestic drama, gains intensified emotional impact from its smaller scale and its highly concentrated action.

Not all of Shakespeare's plays, however, make use of such highly individualized, or unique, or psychologically complex characters as Othello or Hamlet. Comic characters, in particular, often are drawn with a rather broad stroke and remain at the end of the play unchanged from what they were at the beginning. So Shakespeare also dramatizes conflicts that involve not distinctive individuals but those representing a type or attitude. And in the history plays especially he can generate excitement on stage by bringing together men and women with different political and social philosophies. Again and again, Shakespeare demonstrates his agility at balancing a number of different points of view, of giving them voice through his characters, and of dramatizing a plot through this conflict. And in most cases, he seems never to take sides, to indicate a preference, to risk writing propaganda.

Indeed, Shakespeare's evenhandedness and breadth of vision are two of the qualities that mark *As You Like It*. Although the title sounds like a throwaway, what it actually connotes is fitting for this work. Taken literally, the title suggests that the world is to be understood according to our personal predispositions: because of our differing natures, we respond to the same experience in very different ways.

Rosalind, the heroine of this play, has the wisest and richest view of life. But her father, Duke Senior, exiled in the Forest of Arden, seems perfectly content to live there with his faithful courtiers. The positive view of life he extols seems extraordinarily simpleminded, for Duke Senior reminds one of Voltaire's Pangloss. All is for the best: "sweet are the uses of adversity," he argues. His optimism is all-embracing, and his sentiments are always in high gear, ready with a sympathetic emotional response to those difficulties and challenges that in his eyes so sweeten our existence. "Gentleness," compassion, "sacred pity," are for him the marks of genuine humanity since "we are not all alone unhappy."

The Duke's naïvely optimistic view of the human condition is refuted by the melancholy Jaques. His is the voice of cynicism, as emotional and indulgent as the Duke's but directed toward a different end. Jaques's tears are shed not for his fellow man but for the stricken deer. For him, human life is meaningless, only a "strange eventful history," ending in "second childishness and mere oblivion . . . sans everything." In his willfully melancholic mood, he takes perverse delight in railing "against our mistress the world and all our misery." Some of this is posturing, of course; even Jaques admits that his melancholy actually gives him pleasure. But even more important is the fact that in his past he was "as sensual as the brutish sting itself"; as one who "hast been a libertine," the jaundiced view of life that he expresses is typical of a reformed sinner.

With his negative and nihilistic attitude, Jaques is drawn to Touchstone, the clown, who seems to be a fellow traveler. Jaques is in full agreement with Touchstone's moralizing tale:

> He drew a dial from his poke,
> And looking at it with lack-luster eye,

Says very wisely, 'It is ten o'clock.
Thus may we see,' quoth he, 'how this world wags.
'Tis but an hour ago since it was nine,
And after one hour more 'twill be eleven;
And so from hour to hour, we ripe and ripe,
And then, from hour to hour, we rot and rot;
And thereby hangs a tale.'

(II.vii)

But Touchstone's mock-philosophical account is made laughable by its homonyms and language jokes.[28] The word "hour" in Renaissance English sounded like the word "whore," so the clown is really offering not a sermon on the vicissitudes of time but an account of the prognosis of sexual diseases. In effect, the progressive rotting and the pointer drawn from his pocket, which never reaches the erect position of twelve on the clock, describe in a half-joking manner the consequences of profligacy and venereal maladies.

For all his awareness of human weakness and failings, Touchstone never loses his sense of humor; he is not so emotionally self-indulgent as Jaques. The clown is far more dispassionate and realistic. He knows that practical sense will ultimately serve one far better than irritable sarcasm.

Touchstone understands that life requires compromise; absolute values are impossibilities. A shepherd's life can be both pleasant and unpleasant for identical reasons:

. . . in respect of itself, it is a good life; but in respect that it is a shepherd's life, it is naught. In respect that it is solitary, I like it very well; but in respect that it is private, it is a very vile life. Now in respect it is in the fields, it pleaseth me well; but in respect it is not in the court, it is tedious. As it is a spare life, look you it fits my humor well; but as there is no more plenty in it, it goes much against my stomach.

(III.ii)

"As you like it" is a fitting motto for the lesson here. In addition, Touchstone understands that every life has its burdens: "the ox hath his bow, the horse his curb, and the falcon her bells." He will

marry the goatherd Audrey despite her ignorance and foulness—
"sluttishness may come hereafter"—for "man hath his desires"
and the price must be paid.

With his easy good nature and his practical sense, Touchstone is
understandably a favorite with Rosalind, who shares these qualities. Yet she has traits that seem to be lacking in everyone else. Despite her appreciation for the ironies of life and its inconsistencies,
Rosalind has a genuine enthusiasm and idealism that are unique in
the world of the play. Love she knows is sheer madness and "de-
serves as well a dark house and whip as madmen do." Yet, of
course, lovers "are not so punished and cured," for their "lunacy
is so ordinary that the whippers are in love too."

She recognizes the absurd heights of devotion that the shepherd
Silvius claims as a lover par excellence, but while she can smile at
his folly, she can sympathize with his passion: "Alas, poor shepherd! Searching of thy wound,/ I have by hard adventure found
mine own." And she can regard herself with some objectivity, for
Rosalind has the ability to laugh at her own behavior: "Do you not
know that I am a woman? When I think, I must speak." Her attraction to Orlando is so strong that she confesses to her cousin Celia
of feeling great oceans of delight:

> O coz, coz, coz, my pretty little coz, that thou didst know how
> many fathom deep I am in love! But it cannot be sounded. My af-
> fection hath an unknown bottom, like the Bay of Portugal.
>
> (IV.i)

Here is a young woman who knows her own heart, maintains
her sense of humor, and sustains a sound, practical view of life.
When Phebe rejects Silvius's ardent protestations of love, prefer-
ring instead the young boy who is really the disguised Rosalind in
male attire, the heroine offers the misguided Phebe this counsel:

> Down on your knees,
> And thank heaven, fasting, for a good man's love;
> For I must tell you friendly in your ear,
> Sell when you can, you are not for all markets.
>
> (III.v)

Memorable advice and memorably phrased.

The attitudes of Duke Senior, Jaques, Touchstone, and Rosalind range from the more or less sentimental to the more or less realistic, from the more or less optimistic to the more or less cynical. And the plot is simply the mechanism for bringing these and other characters together and engaging them in a series of discussions where their individual views of life can be played off against one another. The charms and limitations of the pastoral convention, with its nostalgia for a lost Eden of youth and innocence—a "golden world"—have never been analyzed on the stage with so much delight, or complexity.

Theater generated by dramatizing opposing views of life can serve as a description for such comedies as *As You Like It* and *The Merchant of Venice*. In some of the history plays, Shakespeare typically invents characters who hold differing political philosophies, in addition to whatever incompatibilities exist among them because of their personalities. The conflict in these works bursts into life when rivals who believe in opposing views meet in an attempt to resolve some issue of national importance. Of all Shakespeare's history plays, *Richard II* presents characters who have perhaps the most distinctive differences in their thinking about the nature of government and rule, differences that make clear the variety of political theories that were current in Shakespeare's time.[29]

The beliefs of Richard II and Bolingbroke concerning the source and basis of royal power, for example, could not be more opposed. Richard thinks of himself as an absolute monarch, chosen by God:

> Not all the water in the rough rude sea
> Can wash the balm off from an anointed king.
> The breath of worldly men cannot depose
> The deputy elected by the Lord.
>
> (III.ii)

Divinely appointed, chosen at birth, he has a lifetime contract to rule, and, what is more, his authority is a law unto itself. When his uncle, John of Gaunt, dies, Richard, needing money, claims posses-

Richard II, 1974, Royal Shakespeare Company, directed by John Barton.
Richard Pasco as Richard II and Ian Richardson as Bolingbroke. Here, in the
abdication scene, the king is about to hand over the crown reluctantly to his cousin.
(*Billy Rose Theatre Collection, The New York Public Library for the Performing
Arts, Astor, Lenox and Tilden Foundations*)

Romeo and Juliet, 1935–36, at the New Theatre (later the Albery), directed by John Gielgud.
Laurence Olivier as Romeo (LEFT); Dame Edith Evans, the Nurse; and John Gielgud (RIGHT), Mercutio. The two men exchanged roles for four months during the course of the run. His performances established Olivier's credentials as a serious and important actor, and this production set the record for the longest continuous run of the play. (*Victoria and Albert Museum*)

From a 2003 Lincoln Center Theatre adaptation of *Henry IV,* Parts I and II, directed by Jack O'Brien. Kevin Kline portrays a jovial Falstaff as he impersonates the king using this "chair as my state, this dagger my sceptre, and this cushion my crown." (*Sara Krulwich*/The New York Times)

Twelfth Night, the 1957–58 Old Vic production, directed by Michael Benthall.
The recognition scene in which Viola (Barbara Jefford) on the left, in her disguise as a boy, is reunited with her twin brother Sebastian (Gerald Harper), facing her on the right. (*Anthony Crickmay, London*)

Hamlet, 1975, The National Theatre at the Old Vic, directed by Peter Hall. In the graveyard scene, Albert Finney as the Prince addresses Yorick's skull. (*Anthony Crickmay, London*)

Macbeth, 1955, Stratford-upon-Avon, directed by Glen Byam Shaw. Laurence Olivier portrayed the king as a brooding man filled with guilt, remorse, and terror. One critic said his was "the best Macbeth since Macbeth." He is seen here with his wife, Vivien Leigh, who played Lady Macbeth. (*Angus McBean/Harvard Theatre Collection*)

King Lear, 1984, Granada Television, directed by Michael Elliott.
Laurence Olivier, in the last Shakespearean role of his distinguished career,
portrayed the aged king as a vulnerable but imperious old man.
(*Granada TV*)

The Tempest, 1995, New York Shakespeare Festival, directed by George C. Wolfe. Patrick Stewart as Prospero. In the act of relinquishing his magic power, he is preparing to break his staff and promising that "deeper than did ever plummet sound / I'll drown my book." (*Michal Daniel*)

sion of the "plate, coin, revenues, and moveables/ Whereof our uncle Gaunt did stand possessed." But Gaunt's estate has a legal heir, his son, Henry Bolingbroke.

York, Richard's last surviving uncle after the death of Gaunt, warns the king that by denying Bolingbroke his inheritance, Richard is dangerously undermining the very basis for his own authority: "for how art thou king/ But by fair sequence and succession?" In addition to the moral and social issues raised by Richard's actions, the seizure of Gaunt's estates will have practical consequences: it will unite opposition to him. York warns him, "You lose a thousand well-disposèd hearts," for many will fear that with this precedent the crown could also appropriate their lands, deny their designated heirs, and leave their children penniless. York's advice is rejected by a king so arrogant, so irresponsible and willful, so spoiled and impractical that he will please himself above all: "Think what you will."

In part, Richard is self-assured because he has always been indulged. He never imagines that his will can be contradicted or his power limited: "Show us the hand of God/ That hath dismissed us from our stewardship," he demands of Bolingbroke. And since God has appointed him absolute ruler, Richard thinks that God will keep him in office: "God for his Richard hath in heavenly pay/ A glorious angel."

When he is forced to undo what he has done, Richard immediately thinks of himself as a deposed or dead king since, according to his definition, kings are not subject to rebuff or refusal. Indeed, Richard seems to surrender the throne almost before it is asked of him: "What you will have, I'll give, and willing too." To his mind, he is not king if he cannot have his way. This explains why the unhappy ruler's first thought is that he has lost his crown, even before that possibility has been raised.

Bolingbroke's political philosophy is very different. He does not deny the possibility of divine involvement in worldly matters, but he hardly gives it primacy of place. He knows that battles are most often won by the side with superior numbers, that public support is an important practical element in sustaining power, and that true intentions do not at all times need to be put into words.

YORK: Take not, good cousin, further than you should,
    Lest you mistake the heavens are over our heads.
BOLINGBROKE: I know it, uncle, and oppose not myself
    Against their will.

(III.iii)

Bolingbroke is suggesting that victory will come to the side that heaven chooses. But his words have even greater implications. In effect, he is implying that he cannot depose the king if heaven does not wish it to happen, and, conversely, that if the king is deposed, then Bolingbroke's success is arguably heaven's will.

The plain truth is that with his army Bolingbroke can force Richard from office. When they confront each other at the turning point of the play, Bolingbroke first offers his "allegiance and true faith of heart," to Richard, only with the proviso that "my banishment repealed/ And lands restored again be freely granted." And, then he somewhat ambiguously adds, "I come but for mine own." Richard has always known that his cousin was ambitious for the crown so the meaning implied here is no surprise to him. With this simple sentence Bolingbroke is indirectly stating that he has come not merely to reclaim his inheritance but to take the throne as well. And Richard has no recourse: "Your own is yours, and I am yours and all."

A third view of politics is also given expression through the words and actions of Richard's uncles, Gaunt and York. Members of an older generation who have sworn fealty to Richard, they clearly feel bound by their oath. Though they may quarrel with him and disapprove of his actions, neither one will actively oppose the king or support those who do. Gaunt's range of action is severely limited:

God's is the quarrel . . .

. . . .

Let heaven revenge, for I may never lift
An angry arm against His minister.

(I.ii)

And York continually defends Richard as well as he can. But when Bolingbroke forces Richard to resign and usurps the throne, York shifts his support to the new monarch even as he pities Richard:

> But heaven hath a hand in these events,
> To whose high will we bound our calm contents.
> To Bolingbroke are we sworn subjects now,
> Whose state and honour I for aye allow.
>
> (V.ii)

In this way he and John of Gaunt are alike. Neither will actively oppose a crowned head, however much they disagree with his policies. Both men hold to the philosophy of passive obedience: the king is "God's substitute/ His deputy anointed in His sight."

Bolingbroke's practical power politics have not only won out over Richard's notion of an absolute, divinely appointed monarch but also brushed aside those like Gaunt and York who practice passive obedience. Yet the threats of what will follow from removing a divinely appointed ruler from the throne also prove true: "The woe's to come. The children yet unborn/ Shall feel this day as sharp to them as thorn." Shakespeare had, in fact, already put on the stage three plays on the Wars of the Roses which were, according to some, a direct consequence of the deposition and ultimate murder of Richard II.

The question of whether a monarch was above the law or governed under the common law was a highly contested one in Shakespeare's time, and the issue of whether subjects had the right to remove their king was so sensitive that the dramatization of Richard's deposition was not included in the early printed versions of the play. (Censorship over the stage was less stringent than over the press.)

Yet the characters who give voice to these attitudes are more than mere mouthpieces for differing philosophies of government and power. Both Richard and Bolingbroke have strong, distinctive personalities. Despite his legitimacy as king, Richard has no political competence. Yet he is a fascinating, poetic, sensitive character who grows in humanity as he loses his kingdom. Bolingbroke, by contrast, is a man of action and expedience; he reveals nothing of an inner life or of an introspective nature. Our interest in the drama is enhanced by the clash between them as well as in their opposing political philosophies.

Whether he develops his characters primarily out of stereotypes or builds them out of historical models, Shakespeare then balances attitudes, points of view, and even political philosophies among the various roles so that his plays and the figures in them have a sense of wholeness or completeness. In these works, the mirror held up to life offers a vivid, wide, and panoramic scene.

6

Mixing Verse and Prose

When he asks his philosophy tutor for help in writing a sophisticated love note, Molière's Bourgeois Gentleman says he wishes to phrase it neither in verse nor in prose. This request leads him to the startling discovery not only that language has limited modes of delivery—his message must be either in one or the other—but also that without knowing it, he has actually been speaking prose for more than forty years. The situation, however, is not quite the same for Shakespeare's characters. Most of them are equally at ease conversing in both verse and prose, and they usually seem unaware which they are speaking. Only once, in fact, does a Shakespearean character call attention to another's mode of language and chastise him for it. In *As You Like It*, Jaques quickly parts company with the lovesick Orlando, "Nay then, God b' wi' you, an you talk in blank verse."

Why Shakespeare chooses to write some scenes in poetry and others in prose is not always self-evident. As a general rule, however, serious moments and tragedies are largely in verse and comic incidents in prose; aristocrats speak in verse, commoners and clowns in prose. Yet in the case of Shakespeare's plays, chronology is also a factor. Some of his early works, such as the *Henry VI* plays, *Richard III, King John*, and *Titus Andronicus,* have a very high percentage of lines in unrhymed iambic pentameter known as blank verse. *Richard II*, composed shortly after these plays, is entirely in rhymed and unrhymed iambic verse: that is, perhaps, as it should be, for Shakespeare's Richard is a man of great imagination and sensitivity. He turns his life and world into a poetic artifact. On the other hand, *King John* is also entirely in verse, but the same justification hardly applies.

In those comedies written near the midpoint of his career, about the turn of the sixteenth century—*As You Like It, Much Ado About Nothing, Twelfth Night,* and *Merry Wives of Windsor*—Shakespeare composes more of the dialogue in prose than in either rhymed or unrhymed verse. *Merry Wives,* in fact, has a higher percentage of its lines in prose than any other Shakespeare play, but that is certainly the appropriate medium for this work, his only bourgeois comedy.

When the action has reached a high point, or when the emotional intensity registers fever pitch, however, Shakespeare usually turns to poetry. That *Macbeth* and *Antony and Cleopatra* contain hardly any lines of prose seems entirely fitting for their stories and the tragedies they dramatize.

When does Shakespeare decide to shift from one mode to another? The mood or the subject seems to dictate how he will present the dialogue. At the end of the first act of *Twelfth Night,* for example, the language suddenly changes gear. We have been hearing the actors speaking prose for more than two hundred lines. Then, quite abruptly, Viola responds to Olivia in blank verse, and the two continue in that medium for their remaining lines in the scene.

During their prose dialogue, Olivia has been taunting the disguised Viola, who is acting as Count Orsino's messenger. Despite her own intense love for the nobleman she serves, Viola is attempting to convey to a sarcastic and scornful Olivia the depth of her employer's adoration. Frustrated by Olivia's absolute indifference to the Count and by her flippant rejection of his affection, Viola, given the chance to respond in hypothetical terms, can describe her own attraction for the Count without openly admitting it. Her words, conveying a sense of her very real passion, are so intense that they immediately arouse in Olivia a new interest not in Orsino but in his young employee. The formerly cold woman unexpectedly finds herself responding to this capacity for love:

OLIVIA: But yet I cannot love him.
   He might have took his answer long ago.
VIOLA: If I did love you in my master's flame,
   With such a suff'ring, such a deadly life,
   In your denial I would find no sense;
   I would not understand it.
OLIVIA: Why, what would you?
VIOLA: Make me a willow cabin at your gate
   And call upon my soul within the house;
   Write loyal cantons of contemnèd love
   And sing them loud even in the dead of night;
   Hallo your name to the reverberate hills
   And make the babbling gossip of the air
   Cry out 'Olivia!' O, you should not rest
   Between the elements of air and earth
   But you should pity me.
OLIVIA: You might do much. What is your
   parentage?

                                     (I.v)

Viola forcefully rejects Olivia's new expression of interest in her—
"Love make his heart of flint that you shall love."

The emotions aroused in this highly complicated situation can
most effectively be conveyed in poetry, for that medium is especially adept at expressing not merely the thoughts of the speaker
but also the degree of feeling that is aroused by those thoughts.
Here we have two women who are both experiencing unrequited
love: Olivia for the disguised Viola, whom she takes to be a handsome young man, and Viola for Orsino. Both are unable to state
their emotions in a direct fashion, for Viola is acting as Orsino's
servant, and Olivia, given her place in society and her gender, cannot play the active pursuer. Yet Viola's devotion to Orsino is stated
in a way that makes it nearly palpable: "you should not rest/ Between the elements of air and earth/ But you should pity me." And
indeed Olivia finds that this youth's direct and sincere expression
of love becomes what she later calls a kind of "enchantment." The
abrupt movement from prose to verse in the scene heightens this
emotionally charged moment. In contrast to the uninflected prose

dialogue that precedes her words, Viola's impassioned speech, so personal and imaginative, is elevated to a different level of thought and feeling by its poetic meter.

Another instance of the differing effects that can be achieved with prose and verse in writing for the stage can be illustrated by comparing the two Forum speeches in *Julius Caesar*.[30] In this case, however, the opposing arguments are placed at the turning point of the action. A great deal is at stake here: an angry Roman populace demands to know why their leader has been murdered. Brutus, speaking for himself and his co-conspirators, expects to "show the reason of our Caesar's death," and he allows Mark Antony, a man who was devoted to Caesar, to address the mob only if he will "not in your funeral speech blame us/ But speak all good you can devise of Caesar/ And say you do't by our permission." Before they hear these orations, the theater audience clearly understands the purposes and intentions of each of the speakers, whose words, by the way, are not derived from classical sources but are totally of Shakespeare's invention.

Brutus is an educated nobleman, a highly respected member of a Roman family whose ancestors once helped bring down a tyrannical government. His participation in the stabbing of Julius Caesar, therefore, lends a degree of legitimacy to the assassination and of credibility to the charge that Caesar would have set himself up as a dictator. Brutus is, perhaps, too well aware of his influence and reputation, for this has made him egotistical, self-assured, and self-righteous. Shakespeare manages to convey all of these qualities of Brutus's character through his language and the way he shapes his argument. The logic of the speech and its rhetorical devices reveal the mind and personality of the speaker.

The prose of Brutus's Forum speech is largely built up out of a succession of parallel phrases—that is, all are of about equal length and with similar word order. For example, his address begins with a call to order:

> . . . hear me for my cause, and be silent that you may hear. Believe
> me for mine honor, and have respect to mine honor, that you may

believe. Censure me in your wisdom, and awake your senses, that
you may the better judge.

(III.ii)

He then moves into his main argument, which is that his love for
Caesar was overcome by his greater love for Rome: "Not that I
loved Caesar less, but that I loved Rome more." The balanced expression of this statement is then rephrased as a rhetorical question:

> Had you rather Caesar were living, and die all slaves, than that Cae-
> sar were dead, to live all free men?

Here, by contrasting the word "slaves" with "free men" and by
reversing the sequence of the verbs (Caesar-living-die; Caesar-
dead-live), Brutus states as an absolute truth the highly questionable assumption that dying as a slave is the only possibly consequence of allowing Caesar to live.

In the next phase of his argument, Brutus stresses the righteousness of his conduct and continues his practice of reversing a sequence. The effect, once again, is to emphasize the inevitability and
appropriateness of what he has done:

> As Caesar loved me, I weep for him; as he was fortunate, I rejoice at
> it; as he was valiant, I honor him; but—as he was ambitious, I slew
> him. There is tears for his love; joy for his fortune; honor for his
> valor; and death for his ambition.

Four of Caesar's qualities are named, and for each of them we
learn Brutus's response. By the way they are presented, Brutus's
behavior appears to be a reasonable and just reaction to Caesar's
nature. The approach, though somewhat stodgy and plodding,
presents an argument that is easily followed and with rather impressive results.

In the final section of his oration, Brutus states his parallel allit-
erative phrases in the form of three rhetorical questions:

> Who is here so base, that would be a bondsman?
> Who is here so rude that would not be a Roman?
> Who is here so vile that will not love his country?

The response to each question is identical: "If any, speak; for him have I offended." And the triple repetition of these words gives them weight. He then pauses to give the crowd time to reaffirm his argument, and he brings his formal oration to a close with a fourth restatement: "Then none have I offended." A sense of finality and justice is admirably achieved.

The cleverness of Brutus's method should not be underestimated. With only his reputation for honor as defense against an accusation that Caesar was ambitious—in itself hardly a mortal sin—and with only that fault to charge him with, Brutus has helped murder the "foremost man of all the world." Unlike Mark Antony who will soon offer specific instances to support his position, Brutus cannot cite examples of Caesar's conduct to support his claim that the man was dangerous. But simply by offering his own responses to his own questions, Brutus manages to persuade the populace to accept his argument.

This is an impressive performance for its skillful shaping of language as well as for its pseudo-logic. But what seems especially remarkable is that Brutus believes he can defend the morality of his murder of Caesar by telling us about Brutus. His favorite words in this oration are "I," "me," and "mine." One can hear the entire speech through to the very exit of Brutus and learn only three lines before he leaves the stage that others may have been involved in the assassination. (Even then his reference, allowing Mark Antony to speak "By our permissions," sounds rather like the royal "we.") Only a man very certain of his rectitude and strong in ego would fail to bolster his defense by naming those public figures who joined with him. Such a man must be either foolish, as Brutus is not, or highly conceited.

Unlike the aloof and aristocratic Brutus, Mark Antony is a crowd-pleaser and a demagogue. He knows enough about mob mentality to sway his listeners, and he understands that it is far easier to win them over by emotional appeals than by reason or logical argument. Naturally, he speaks in blank verse, the language of feeling and heightened emotion.

Antony's speech falls into several stages. He begins with a plea for attention and an indirect attack on his opponents:

> The noble Brutus
> Hath told you Caesar was ambitious.
> If it were so, it was a grievous fault,
> And grievously hath Caesar answered it.

His rebuttal then starts with a personal remembrance—"He was my friend, faithful and just to me"—and recounts three positive examples of Caesar's character. Actually, only the third example, his rejection of a "kingly crown," counters the charge of ambition.

This section of the oration then ends with a display of personal emotion and an appeal for sympathy: "You all did love him once. . . ." Antony claims to require time to regain his composure ("Bear with me"); and this pause conveniently affords him a chance to observe how his remarks are affecting his audience and to give them a chance to react to his words.

Antony resumes his speech by continuing his indirect attack on the conspirators. And he has saved his strongest point for last: Caesar's will. He teases and taunts the crowd by telling it that the dead man's will profits them directly, but he refuses to read the document.

Antony can be certain the mob will listen to him; their own self-interest will serve as an especially strong motive to hold their attention. So Antony now tells them they will not learn what they have gained from Caesar until they have seen his body and heard an account of the murder. His narration of the death of Caesar is powerful, graphic and specific, and quite remarkable since he was not present at the time. By his emotional account of Caesar's death and by displaying the mangled body, Antony thoroughly discredits the conspirators. His description of the murder ends with his first direct attack on them: it was a deed of "bloody treason."

With the mob frenzied and the direct assault on his enemies now underway, Antony next works to assure their support. He contrasts his opponents, sarcastically calling them "wise and honorable" men, with himself, "a plain blunt man." He presents himself as a speaker who improvises his remarks, whose modesty and simple language will find a responsive chord among his hearers: "I only speak right on./ I tell you that which you yourselves do know."

The infuriated populace is ready to fly to vengeance. Antony re-
strains them first in order to arm them against his opponents' verbal cleverness who "will, no doubt, with reasons answer you." Yet
he leaves them firmly committed to purely emotional, irrational responses: "rise and mutiny." Again, he insists that they remain to
hear Caesar's will. One might think that the pitch of emotion
would be lost, that the unthinking passion of their anger against
Brutus and his fellows would be dissipated by the details of Caesar's will. But Antony knows that the bequests will ultimately
prove to his own advantage: the mob will always remember what
they have gained from the man whose murderers they will punish.
And so he reads to them of Caesar's munificence as though that
were the final proof against the charge of ambition.

Confirmed in their intent to seek instant revenge, the mob is at
last released to mischief: "Here was a Caesar! When comes such
another?" His speech has had exactly the effect he desired: "Domestic fury and fierce civil strife." "Blood and destruction" were
his prophecy over the body of Caesar, and his words have now accomplished his purpose. The traitors' houses will be burned instantly, and, in the next scene, the frenzied mob will tear the
innocent poet Cinna limb from limb.

The two different approaches to language demonstrated in these
speeches reflect the different personalities of the two orators. Brutus, with his trust in reason and the reasonableness of men, believes
he can persuade others by logic and argument—even when the
logic is weak and the argument faulty. His highly stylized literary
mode befits a conservative aristocrat who clearly thinks himself
unexcelled in intelligence and reputation. After all, he even uses his
high opinion of himself as evidence of his rectitude and good sense.
By contrast, Antony is a rabble-rouser. Using irony and repetition
in his speech, he appeals to the emotions of his audience and to
their own self-interst in order to win them over to his side.

By juxtaposing these two very differently constructed orations,
Shakespeare is delighting his audience, alert to the techniques of
rhetoric, sensitive to language, and appreciative of its skillful ma-
nipulation. The playwright demonstrates his virtuosity by his ability to argue both sides of the case; to set one address in prose, the

other in verse; and to adopt a different but appropriate set of rhetorical principles for each speaker.

Shakespeare's preeminence as a poet may lead us to undervalue how well he wrote prose.[31] Brutus's oration demonstrates Shakespeare's easy control over prose speech. Some of his lines demonstrate the artfulness of matching balanced phrases in a series and creating these phrases with parallel word order—"hear me for . . . and . . . that"; "Believe me for . . . and . . . that"; "Censure me in . . . and . . . that." And he adds a degree of power and finality by the use of incremental repetition—reiterating a phrase such as "If any, speak; for him have I offended" three times, then closing with the line: "Then none have I offended." Such rhetoric devices help build the argument to a forceful climax. And in all of this, the logical basis for the speaker's reactions is made eminently clear.

Shakespeare could write comic as well as serious prose. Beatrice, at the opening of Act II of *Much Ado About Nothing*, teasingly explains why no man suits her: "He that hath a beard is more than a youth, and he that hath no beard is less than a man; and he that is more than a youth is not for me; and he that is less than a man, I am not for him." The rhythmic nature of the sentence, the rhetorical reversals that it proposes, and Shakespeare's ability to add metaphor and imagery at any time make it easily compatible with both rhymed and unrhymed verse. Indeed, often one cannot distinguish in the hearing whether the lines are written as prose or blank verse.

Although he continually demonstrates his easy command of both verse and prose, Shakespeare is aware that at times neither one is appropriate. A character's silence can become expressive, for wordlessness can also convey emotional responses. When Claudio in *Much Ado About Nothing* suddenly realizes that his initial fears were mistaken and, as promised, his marriage proposal was actually brokered for him by Don Pedro, the prospective bridegroom is so surprised by this happy turn of events that he is at a loss for words. He does not answer when a joyful response to the good tidings is clearly in order. Beatrice nudges him to react to the news, prompting him with her line: "Speak, Count, 'tis your cue." And when at last he does respond, his language acknowledges how he has been taken aback: "Silence is the perfectest herald of joy."

Shock and surprise can take one's words away, as is the case with Claudio. But silence can also be a trait of the bashful and shy. It is this quality that marks Orlando, the handsome wrestler who has attracted Rosalind's attention in the first act of *As You Like It*. Celia addresses him first after he has won the match:

> CELIA: Sir, you have well deserved;
>   If you do keep promises in love
>   But justly as you have exceeded all promise,
>   Your mistress shall be happy.
> ROSALIND: Gentleman,
>   [Gives chain.]
>   Wear this for me, one out of suits with fortune,
>   That could give more but that her hand lacks means.
>   Shall we go, coz?
> CELIA: Ay, Fare you well, fair gentleman.
>
> (I.ii)

Orlando misses his cue, which is to thank Celia for her good wishes and Rosalind for her unexpected gift of the ornamental chain. They stand waiting for him to say something, but since he stands before them tongue-tied and embarrassed, Rosalind finally turns to Celia with her line, "Shall we go, coz?" As they move away, Orlando speaks in an aside:

> Can I not say 'I thank you'? My better spirits
> Are all thrown down, and that which here stands up
> Is but a quintain, a mere lifeless block.

Rosalind is so reluctant to leave the young man that she makes another try to engage him in conversation. She turns to Celia with the false claim:

> He calls us back. My pride fell with my fortunes;
> I'll ask him what he would. Did you call, sir?
> Sir, you have wrestled well, and overthrown
> More than your enemies.

Still, Orlando is unable to return the compliment or acknowledge her attention. Finally, Celia turns to Rosalind:

> Will you go, coz?
> ROSALIND: Have with you. Fare you well.

When the two have left the stage, Orlando then berates himself for his timidity:

> What passion hangs these weights upon my tongue?
> I cannot speak to her, yet she urged conference.

His reticence is a basic trait of his personality. Orlando, who is un-educated and unpolished, lacks courtliness or elegant manners. His schooling has been nature; honesty and forthrightness are his basic qualities. Naturally, he finds the challenge of conversing socially with the two young, well-bred women to be slightly intimidating. His appeal is in his simplicity and shyness, not always the easiest traits to communicate from the stage. No wonder Sir Laurence Olivier, one of the foremost Shakespearean actors of his genera-tion, called the role of Orlando "the perfect part for a stick."

Elsewhere, Shakespeare uses a long stage silence as a means of setting off an important turning point in the action. In *Coriolanus*, the hero, after listening to a moving speech from his very powerful mother, thinks about the decision he must make—to remain with the Volscians and fight against his native city or to break his word to them and go back to Rome. According to the stage direction, Coriolanus turns to Volumnia and "holds her by the hand, silent." He knows that by yielding to his mother and returning to Rome, his life is put in jeopardy, but he also knows that he has never been capable of refusing her:

> O mother, mother! O
> You have won a happy victory to Rome;
> But for your son—believe it, O believe it!—
> Most dangerously have you with him prevailed,
> If not most mortal to him. But let it come.
>
> (V.iii)

In each of these three instances, Shakespeare uses silence as a means of conveying a character's reaction to the dramatic situation—surprise, embarrassment, indecision. Shakespeare, a master of both verse and prose, understands that at certain times the very absence of words can reveal a character's personality, temperament, or emotion in a psychologically truthful and dramatically effective way.

Shakespeare's genius as a writer of blank verse developed over the course of his career. At different times he seems to have been interested in achieving different effects. But as we might expect, in general his growth reflected his practical experience in the theater, in the shaping of poetic dialogue into a dramatic rather than a lyric medium. In his earlier work, he often includes set pieces of descriptive writing. Oberon's delightful account of the time Cupid's arrow missed its target is an example that occurs early in the second act of *A Midsummer Night's Dream*:

> That very time I saw (but thou couldst not)
> Flying between the cold moon and the earth
> Cupid, all armed. A certain aim he took
> At a fair vestal, thronèd in the west,
> And loosed his love-shaft smartly from his bow,
> As it should pierce a hundred thousand hearts.
> But I might see young Cupid's fiery shaft
> Quenched in the chaste beams of the wat'ry moon
> And the imperial vot'ress passèd on,
> In maiden meditation, fancy-free.
>
> (II.i)

This is highly imaginative scene painting, doubtless adding color to an Elizabethan acting company's performance on a bare stage. But though enchanting, it is irrelevant. Oberon's words, no doubt, help sustain the fanciful world of the play, but they make no real contribution to plot or character.

In his later works, Shakespeare does not often allow himself the indulgence of spinning wonderful lyric fancies. When in *King Lear* Edgar describes the staggering perspective he sees from the brink of a cliff at Dover—"And dizzy 'tis to cast one's eyes so low"—his words are a necessary description for his blind father. Moreover, his detailed version of what lies below the chalk cliff is completely imagined, for the two men are actually standing on flat ground. Edgar hopes to overcome his father's despair by convincing him that his suicide attempt is wrong, that "Thy life's a miracle."

The difference between lyric and dramatic blank verse can perhaps best be demonstrated by comparing two similar moments. In *Romeo and Juliet*, a rather early work, and *King Lear*, a fully mature one, two tragic heroes confront the death of those they love. Yet in their grief the two men use language in such very different ways that their responses are remarkably dissimilar. Curiously enough, Romeo speaks as one who is formally addressing himself rather than expressing what he feels. This sense of a divided ego seems rather to distance him from the immediacy of what he confronts. His language is highly rhetorical; striving for pathos, the apostrophes and imperatives make his lines sound elevated but artificial.

> Eyes, look your last!
> Arms, take your last embrace! And lips, O you
> The doors of breath, seal with a righteous kiss
> A dateless bargain to engrossing death!
> Come bitter conduct; come, unsavory guide!
>
> (V.iii)

All this is very well as poetry, but no individual, deeply personal and distinctive response finds expression here. On the other hand, King Lear's words are those of an angry, grief-stricken man in great torment, feeling the absolute void caused by his daughter's death:

> Howl, howl, howl, howl! O, you are men of stones!
> Had I your tongues and eyes, I'd use them so
> That heaven's vault should crack:
>   She's gone for ever.
> I know when one is dead and when one lives;
> She's dead as earth.
>
> (V.iii)

The tender pathos of Romeo, who is telling himself what to do, makes for fine lyric writing, but his words hardly convey the heartbreaking emotion one hears in the old man's lines. By contrast, Lear's intense suffering and loss find expression in simple, powerful language that directly communicates what he so deeply feels. Well performed, the effect on the spectator can be overwhelming.

Dramatic dialogue written in rhyme is hardly so flexible a medium as blank verse. Yet Shakespeare's plays offer examples of rhymed verse written in stanzas for singing, of various rhyming patterns including the sonnet form, and of rhyming jingles and doggerel. *Love's Labour's Lost* contains a whole series of sonnets delivered by rhapsodic young men, but perhaps the most subtle instance occurs in *Romeo and Juliet*, when the two lovers speak the very first words that they exchange. They are youthful spirits so in tune with one another that they converse in a perfectly shared sonnet:

> ROMEO:
>   If I profane with my unworthiest hand
>   This holy shrine, the gentle sin is this;
>   My lips, two blushing pilgrims, ready stand
>   To smooth that rough touch with a tender kiss.
> JULIET:
>   Good pilgrim, you do wrong your hand too much,
>   Which mannerly devotion shows in this;
>   For saints have hands that pilgrims' hands do touch,
>   And palm to palm is holy palmers' kiss.
> ROMEO:
>   Have not saints lips, and holy palmers too?
> JULIET:
>   Ay, pilgrim, lips that they must use in prayer.
> ROMEO:
>   O, then, dear saint, let lips do what hands do!
>   They pray; grant thou, lest faith turn to despair.
> JULIET:
>   Saints do not move, though grant for prayers' sake.
> ROMEO:
>   Then move not while my prayer's effect I take.

                                                                        (I.v)

And with that, he kisses her.

Their perfect matching of each other's lines and the ease with which they sustain the metaphor—Romeo, the pilgrim, is seeking to have his prayers answered at the shrine of the saint, Juliet—are proof of how ideal and extraordinary is this moment. The audience surely could not be fully conscious that they were hearing a Shakespearean sonnet; the playwright must have fashioned it simply for the pleasure of meeting the challenge of writing one in dialogue form. Perhaps he was working on his own sonnet sequence at the time so his pen found its way into that demanding form with special ease. But the effort was motivated essentially by self-satisfaction, by a desire to prove one's own absolute control over language, dramatic situation, and character while phrasing it in a complex poetic structure.

Shakespeare's astonishing language skill could be a liability. If he did not rein in his powerful ingenuity he could be too clever for his hearers, placing his own extraordinary inventiveness above the primary need for dramatizing character, plot, and situation. The opening speech of *Love's Labour's Lost* is an example of language that comes near straining the listener with the richness of its imagery and the complexity of its rhetoric.[32] In his address to his closest friends, the young King Ferdinand exhorts them to join him for three years in the pursuit of fame by living a life apart, forming a little academy exclusively devoted to study:

> When, spite of cormorant devouring Time,
> Th'endeavor of this present breath may buy
> That honor which shall bate his scythe's keen edge
> And make us heirs of all eternity.

(I.i)

Ferdinand argues that only fame can give one lasting recognition. To use his rather elaborate metaphor: an enduring reputation alone ("honor") can dull ("bate") the sharp blade ("keen edge") of time ("devouring Time"), which consumes ("cormorant devouring") or mows down (with his "scythe's keen edge") every living thing.

Ferdinand's intentions may be conveyed in highly imaginative language, but the word games played here are even more extreme. The word "breath" leads Shakespeare to pun on the word "scythe's," which, in Elizabethan English, could pass as a homonym for "sighs." And since puns are often irresistible occasions for proving his extravagant agility with words, Shakespeare gives us a three-base hit with the combination: "breath"; "scythe's"/sighs; and "heirs"/airs. The implied contrast of respiration, ephemeral and insubstantial, with eternal fame places the King's pursuit rather in the realm of the impossible or the fanciful. But the point is not lost. Although the action throughout the next five acts is often raucous and farcical, the play ends with a touching mixture of the comic and the serious as we witness a pageant of the Worthies, i.e., those men thought deserving of eternal fame, such as "Hector of Troy," "Pompey the Great," "Alexander," "Hercules," "Judas Maccabaeus."

The tension in resolving the question of the proper aim of life, whether to live it as an insubstantial pageant or in pursuit of the "bubble reputation," is finally swept aside as the men succumb to nature, to feminine beauty, to desire. And even if the poetry may be overly dense at times and the joy in the language games somewhat forced, the audience can still grasp the coherence of the whole, the unity of the action. Naturally, those more sensitive to rhetoric may take great pleasure in the inventiveness of the language, but one need not have the ear of a poet to enjoy watching how love's labor's lost.

Shakespeare makes rather heavy use of rhyme throughout *Love's Labour's Lost* and *A Midsummer Night's Dream* in particular. But in all of his plays, the heroic couplet—two rhyming, ten-syllable lines of alternating stressed and unstressed syllables (iambic pentameter)—is the form of rhymed dialogue most often found. These couplets frequently are the closing lines of a scene. The rhyme sounds a note of finality, bringing a sense of closure to the action. Interestingly enough, that rhyme sound may also have served as an aural clue to the bookholder or prompter standing backstage, who would need to know when to begin the next scene by sending out

before the audience the actors waiting offstage. Two brief examples
will make the effect clear. In *Henry IV, Part One*, the King is anx-
ious to complete his plans to confront the rebels and put down
their attempt to overthrow him. He tells Hal and Sir Walter Blunt:

> Our hands are full of business. Let's away:
> Advantage feeds him fat while men delay.
>
> (III.ii)

The three actors exit and, as they leave, the next scene begins with
Falstaff and his sidekick Bardolph making their entrance. In *Hamlet*, at the end of Act I, the prince, having sworn to revenge his
father's murder, brings the scene to a close with a couplet and leads
those with him off the stage:

> The time is out of joint. O cursèd spite
> That ever I was born to set it right.
> Nay, come let's go together.
>
> (I.v)

To help the audience in the theater distinguish between the world
of the play and occasional moments in the performance that are
outside of it—songs, incantations, playlets within the play—
Shakespeare often alters his language and his poetic line. For example, in some cases when he ends a play with an appeal for applause,
known as a plaudite, Shakespeare composes the actor's lines in
rhyme and in iambic tetrameter, that is, four beats to the line (not
iambic pentameter, a five-beat line). Both *A Midsummer Night's
Dream* and *The Tempest* end in this manner. The last words of *A
Midsummer Night's Dream*, addressed directly to the audience, belong to Puck, who is known as Robin Goodfellow:

> Give me your hands, if we be friends,
> And Robin shall restore amends.
>
> (V.i)

And in *The Tempest*, the magician Prospero, who has pardoned his
enemies, asks the same from the theater audience:

As you from crimes would pardoned be,
Let your indulgence set me free.

(Epilogue)

This formal appeal for applause is a convention adopted from
Roman comedy; and to distinguish this moment the actor, though
in costume, steps out of character to address the audience.

Plaudites, it should be noted, can be written in prose as well as
verse. *As You Like It* concludes with the boy actor playing Rosalind, the protagonist, making a charming direct appeal to the men
and women in the audience for their approval:

> I charge you, O women, for the love you bear to men, to like as much
> of this play as please you; and I charge you, O men, for the love you
> bear to women (as I perceive by your simp'ring none of you hates
> them), that between you and the women the play may please. If I were
> a woman, I would kiss as many of you as had beards that pleased me,
> complexions that liked me, and breaths that I defied not; and I am
> sure, as many as have good beards, or good faces, or sweet breaths,
> will, for my kind offer, when I make curtsy, bid me farewell.

(Epilogue)

Shakespeare's verse is also distinctive for its extensive incorporation of common adages or axioms, proverbial sayings or saws: "the
apparel oft proclaims the man," (*Hamlet*) or "Lions make leopards
tame./ Yea, but not change his spots!" (*Richard II*). This practice
gives the playwright's lines a frequent grounding in everyday
thoughts and words, a counterbalance to the occasional extrava-
gance of his poetic invention. It adds to our sense that Shakespeare
has absorbed the wisdom of our common knowledge; that the nor-
mal and the natural are also a part of what we see on stage; that,
despite its artifices, the drama unfolding before us will fundamentally reflect how we react and respond to our shared experiences.

Finally, Shakespeare's manner of expressing his thoughts also
has been deeply colored by both the Old and the New Testa-
ments.[33] Often he is not directly quoting from the Bible, but its
wording has helped shape the formulation of his language whether
he is writing blank verse or prose. Among his plays, *The Merchant*

of Venice and *Measure for Measure* are especially indebted to the Bible for their phrasing. When a young friend tells Antonio, the melancholy merchant of Venice, "You have too much respect upon the world;/ They lose it that do buy it with much care," he is paraphrasing Matthew 16: "For what is a man profited, if he shall gain the whole world, and lose his own soul?" In the same play, when Portia compares the "quality of mercy" to the "gentle rain from heaven," Shakespeare may well have in the back of his mind the words of Ecclesiasticus 35: "Mercy is seasonable in the time of affliction,/ As clouds of rain in the time of drought." And even in choosing *Measure for Measure* as the title for his play, Shakespeare is drawing again on the Gospel of Matthew: "With what measure ye mete, it shall be measured to you again."

That biblical phrases have permeated Shakespeare's thought is hardly surprising since in his day attendance at Sunday church services was compulsory—absenteeism was fined. Moreover, by incorporating sentiments and language from the Bible into his plays, Shakespeare can draw his audience more readily into the world of his plays, for this is a world that is not alien to their own.

How does Shakespeare decide when to use which instrument—blank verse, rhyme, prose—what pitch to play it in, how loudly to sound it, and with what accompaniment? An infallible ear, his genius as an artist, an intuitive sense of how to achieve a desired effect, his experience in the theater: these are all reasonable and probably valid explanations. Success of this kind cannot be accomplished through conscious, rational thought; aristocratic blood lines; rank; worldly privilege; or formal education. Shakespeare completely immersed himself in the creative process. How else could he have accomplished what the poet John Keats heard in the language of *King Lear*: "the fierce dispute/ Betwixt damnation and impassion'd clay."[34]

7

Incorporating Theatrical Devices

To provide his works with unexpected and innovative moments, Shakespeare makes use of a number of theatrical devices that enhance the popular appeal of his plays. Dreams are wondrously enacted; eavesdropping scenes advance both plot and character; plays have playlets performed as a part of the action; mimed sequences are incorporated; pageants unfold; extravagant spectacles and entertainments, music and songs all add excitement and variety to the unfolding of the drama. Some of these scenes are largely symbolic, others highly theatrical, but analyzing specific examples will demonstrate how these bring variety and freshness to Shakespeare's dramatization of a story and its characters. Especially remarkable in this survey is the way that in his mature writing Shakespeare reworks conventional playhouse devices so they serve a multitude of new purposes.

To start with the least dramatic example, in *Richard II* Shakespeare actually stages a literary metaphor. At the close of the third act, he invents a scene in which the Queen and her ladies-in-waiting listen to the Duke of York's gardeners discussing their work. What is enacted in this embellishment of the plot is the implied comparison of England as garden; neither character nor story is developed. The clipping and weeding that the gardeners vigorously undertake to maintain "law and form and due proportion," are a way of stressing "what pity is it" that Richard "had not so trimmed and dressed his land/ As we this." The care they take in cultivating the land is set in sharp contrast to the present situation in Richard's own kingdom, a "sea-walled garden":

> . . . full of weeds, her fairest flowers choked up,
> Her fruit trees all unprimed, her hedges ruined,
> Her knots disordered, and her wholesome herbs
> Swarming with caterpillars.
>
> (III.iv)

The metaphor of England-as-garden, established earlier when John of Gaunt called his country "this other Eden," is actualized on stage. Gardening and land management are analogized with responsible governing and political administration. At the close of the scene, the gardener's news of the fall of Richard, now "in the mighty hold/ Of Bolingbroke," is compared by the Queen to "a second fall of cursed man." Richard's failure to rule properly is presented as a failure to act in a manner consistent with natural principles, and like Adam, the first gardener, Richard will lose paradise and face death.

This scene is surely more poetic than theatrical, but that is appropriate in this play, which is written entirely in verse. Although it hardly furthers the action or develops the characters, it accomplishes several other useful purposes: it provides an opportunity to reassert the nature imagery that is dominant in the work; it restates in a new way the reasons for Richard's failure as a king; and it establishes the mood of sorrow and melancholy that from this point will characterize the rest of the action.

Yet scenes which dramatize a poetic metaphor will seldom prove as thrilling as those that stage a dream sequence. As Shakespeare would have known from medieval narratives and earlier dramas, on these occasions a dramatist can enact omens, portents, and proofs of private guilt. Often in these dream scenes the resources of the stage are fully engaged. In *Cymbeline*, the hero, Posthumus, falls asleep. To the sound of solemn music, a dream is then enacted in which the ghosts of his family implore Jupiter for help, and, in a bit of spectacular staging, the god "descends in thunder and lightning, sitting upon an eagle: he throws a thunderbolt. The Ghosts fall on their knees." Jupiter assures Posthumus's family that their son will prosper, and indeed, as we might anticipate, all things turn out as the god predicts. By declaring that his ways are inscrutable and that "whom best I love I cross," Jupiter offers an explanation of why bad things happen to good people. Then with a flourish he "ascends" into the ceiling over the stage; as one of the ghosts remarks, "The marble pavement closes, he is enter'd/ His radiant roof." The machinery for lowering and raising actors to the stage, its pulley noises camouflaged by music, had long been in use, and in this play its employment is appropriate as a part of the tragicomedy of the action, full of surprises and reversals.

Another example of an elaborately staged vision scene that provides consolation to the sleeper occurs in *Henry VIII*. While "sad and solemn music" is played, the dying Queen Katherine experiences a dream in which six white-dressed dancers offer her wreaths of "bays or palms." Again, the action is reassuring and, once awake, Katherine interprets it as a promise of "eternal happiness." Since this marks her last appearance in the play, the vision makes clear that the unhappy Queen will ultimately find her just reward in the next life.

Not all dreamers find consolation and happiness in their dreams nor do all dream visions have such elaborate special staging requirements. Richard III before his defeat and death in the battle of Bosworth Field is visited in his sleep by the ghosts of eight of his victims. These spirits offer encouragement to his opponent in the coming fight and urge him to "despair and die." Their appearance establishes the weight of guilt that is crushing Richard—"my conscience . . . condemns me for a villain"—and reminds the audience of the sequence of murders that brought him to the crown. The action here is similar to the moment in *Julius Caesar*, a play written well after *Richard III*, when Caesar's ghost, identifying himself as "thy evil spirit," appears to a sleepy Brutus "to tell thee thou shalt see me at Philippi." The appearance of the ghost is proof of what

Brutus realizes just before his own death: "O Julius Caesar, thou art mighty yet!/ Thy spirit walks abroad and turns our swords/ Into our own proper entrails."

Our last example of a sleeper who experiences another level of experience occurs in the odd prologue or induction to *The Taming of the Shrew*. In the opening moments of this play the inebriated tinker, Christopher Sly, is the victim of a practical joke. His clothes and appearance are altered so that when he awakens from his drunken stupor he is told that he is a member of the landed gentry. In this new incarnation as Lord Christopher he witnesses the shrew-taming play, for he is told that its "mirth and merriment" will help cure him of his "former malady," the fifteen-year delirium he suffered when he thought himself a poor tinker. As the play of the taming of the shrew gets under way, a sleepy Lord Christopher Sly is heard from only once more, very briefly at the end of the first scene when he remarks that though "'tis an excellent piece of work . . . would't were done."

The epilogue that might be expected to round out the illusionary life of the poor tinker is missing, or was never written, or belongs to another treatment of the story somehow related to this. In any case, all that can be understood from this brief opening episode that relates it to the shrew-taming story is that one's character can be transformed by believing in the transformation and by acting the part.

The issues raised by the practical joke, however, are important in Shakespeare's thinking. His plays often question the nature of reality, or dramatize the challenge of distinguishing between the illusory and the actual, between what one dreamed and what one experienced awake. For a poet, playwright, and actor—a professional concerned with creating an imaginative world of play and pretending—such considerations must have been frequently in his thoughts. In his mind the links that connect the real and the imagined are very strong and the boundary between them difficult to draw. As he says in *A Midsummer Night's Dream*:

> Such tricks hath strong imagination
> That, if it would but apprehend some joy,

It comprehends some bringer of that joy;
Or in the night, imagining some fear,
How easy is a bush supposed a bear!

(V.i)

The Christopher Sly induction or prologue, although it appears fragmentary and rather unsatisfactory, bears on these characteristically Shakespearean issues.

Eavesdropping scenes also enhance the development of plot and character. Such moments occur when one or more characters overhear others onstage but remain unseen by them. The theatrical effectiveness of such moments was established by the writers of Roman comedy, but no playwright in the creation of comedies or tragedies devised eavesdropping scenes with as much frequency, variety, and inventiveness as Shakespeare, or invested them with as much psychological complexity, or handled them with as much theatrical brilliance. Indeed, analyzing the multiple ways that Shakespeare stages this device and the uses he makes of it demonstrates his astonishing creative resourcefulness.

Surely one of the prime reasons for the frequency of such scenes in Shakespeare's works is that they make for good theater. The audience is witness to an action that is more or less underhanded, a bit of trickery with consequences that are open to both comic and tragic possibilities. And as the action unfolds, the emotional investment of the audience is heightened either by their sympathy for those being duped or by their identification with the duper. Moreover, along with the eavesdropper, those in the audience now know facts that others onstage do not know, the perfect situation for dramatic irony. And if the eavesdropper speaks directly to the audience in a private and confidential manner, the members of the audience become collaborators, secret sharers in the act of overhearing a private conversation or the most personal of confessions. In sum, from a playwright's point of view, eavesdropping scenes are an effective way of developing both plot and character while involving the spectator in the action.

Perhaps the simplest and best-known example of accidental or unintentional eavesdropping in the Shakespeare canon occurs in

Romeo and Juliet (II.iii). Romeo, drawn by his attraction to the young Capulet, stands in darkness under Juliet's balcony when by chance she speaks aloud of her love for the young Montague she has just met. After listening to her confess her feelings to the night air, he steps forward, reveals himself, and acknowledges his love for her.

Never mind that Juliet's private thoughts are so publicly addressed they can be overheard by a love-struck intruder. The essential point is the honesty and forthrightness of her words. Their candor is a refreshing contrast to the earlier language of Romeo and his friends whose artificial, elaborate Petrarchan conceits of frustration and denial express only the convention, to use Keats's words, of the forever young, forever panting.

The information gained inadvertently by eavesdropping enables Romeo and Juliet in very little time to exchange their vows of love with simple directness: "farewell, compliment." Shakespeare makes the device serve both plot and character; he has not only greatly accelerated the action of the play but also dramatized the tenderness and honesty of his teenage lovers.

In the interests of love, eavesdropping also occurs in *Love's Labour's Lost*, but with comic results. In IV.iii the audience watches as the four young men of the play, who have vowed to lead an ascetic and intellectual life, discover that they all are smitten. No sooner has Berowne in soliloquy admitted that he has broken his oath by loving Rosaline, than the King enters confessing that despite himself, he cannot help adoring the Princess of France. Berowne, hidden, overhears the King read a love lyric to the woman who has captured his heart. Longaville, the third oath-breaker, next appears "with several papers"; the King conceals himself, and now both he and Berowne separately listen to the reading of still another sonnet professing love. Then Dumain, the fourth and last, makes his entrance revealing, once again through a literary effort, his affection for Kate, unaware that he is overheard by his three hidden companions.

This windup toy now unwinds: Longaville, indignant, confronts Dumain on his shocking admission; the King, professing innocence, steps forward to scold Longaville for being guilty of the same offense for which he just berated Dumain; and at last Berowne comes out of hiding to confront the King with his hypocrisy and all of them with their weakness. The climax, the final revelation, occurs when Berowne's messenger, carrying his sonnet to Rosaline, mistakenly delivers it to the King. The cat is now out of the bag, and the eavesdropping stakes have been raised by a multiple of three.

A more serious example of intentional eavesdropping occurs in *Measure for Measure*. At this request—"Bring me to hear them speak, [but] where I may be conceal'd"—the Duke is placed within earshot of the sister–brother conference in which Isabella reports to Claudio that if she will sleep with Angelo, the new Deputy, he has offered to spare Claudio's life. Learning that he might be saved, Claudio pleads with Isabella to agree to this bargain. The behavior of both the Deputy and Claudio must be deeply shocking to the Duke. It can hardly be what he anticipated; and, indeed, resolving the difficulties he has uncovered becomes in large measure the substance of the rest of the play.

Surely one of the most memorable and fully developed examples in the category of deliberate or planned eavesdropping occurs in *Twelfth Night* (II.v). Here Malvolio, Olivia's steward, convinced by Maria's forged letter that his employer loves him, struts about in the full blush of his self-conceit, his behavior evoking a variety of responses from his hidden observers, Maria, Sir Toby, Sir Andrew, and Fabian. The principle involved seems to be that the greater the number of sharers and the greater the variety of their reactions, the greater the joy generated by the enterprise. Moreover, since we delight in their eavesdropping and in their comments on Malvolio's pomposity, we become participants in the scheme. Our sense of involvement enhances our feeling of participation in the laughter, scorn, and enjoyment of those looking on.

A still more complicated instance of deliberate eavesdropping occurs when the eavesdroppers are not hidden in a box-tree like Maria and her associates but remain completely invisible. In *A Midsummer Night's Dream*, Oberon, unseen and silent, overhears the quarrel of young Demetrius and Helena; and Puck, "his jester and lieutenant," invisible to mortal sight like all the fairies, listens to the Athenian workers rehearsing their play in the forest. The real payoff to these simple eavesdropping incidents comes in the comic confusion that follows when, because of Puck's intercession, the Fairy King and his mischievous assistant can watch with amusement as the four distraught lovers chase one another, or as Titania, the Fairy Queen, dotes "in extremity" on the asinine Bottom. Since moral criteria applied to human behavior can hardly be used to judge these impish fairies "of another sort," we are encouraged against all logic to believe that Oberon delights to be cuckolded by the ass-headed Bottom, or that Titania is not resentful of her husband's punishment.

In the action of *Much Ado About Nothing*, Shakespeare offers further variations on eavesdropping scenes. In some instances the eavesdropping is intentional and malicious; in others it is unintentional and benevolent. In some, what is heard is misunderstood; in others the information gained is correctly appreciated. In some cases, eavesdropping, or "noting," comes to "nothing," but in others it has potentially serious consequences. Indeed, the action of this play almost seems structured out of examples of different sorts of eavesdropping dramatized in rapid succession.

The episode that forms the crisis of the action involves a deliberately planned eavesdropping incident that occurs offstage—Claudio and the Prince report that they saw Hero "talk with a ruffian at her chamber-window" the night before her wedding. The truth of what has happened, the potential reversal of this libel, occurs in an onstage, accidental eavesdropping episode when the cruel fraud is discovered. As the night watchmen make their rounds they quite literally eavesdrop, since by chance they overhear the conversation of Borachio and Conrade who are speaking under an eave, "for it drizzles rain." What Dogberry, the Master Constable, and his men hear is Borachio's boast of his recent offstage wooing of Margaret "by the name of Hero . . . at her mistress' chamber-window" in such a way that "the Prince [and] Claudio . . . saw afar off in the orchard this amiable encounter." In this way Hero was made to appear to take a lover the very night before her wedding. In effect, in this scene Shakespeare is actually dramatizing eavesdroppers who, in the act of eavesdropping, hear an account of an incident of eavesdropping! After the Watch have learned of the scheme to slander Hero, they manage, despite their obtuseness, to arrest these "two aspicious persons" and eventually expose their deceit.

Also unusual is the fact that in Borachio's tale two of the eavesdroppers, the Prince and Claudio, are themselves tricked. This is very different from what happens most often, for the eavesdropper, his secrecy giving him an advantage, is usually the one who does the tricking. Yet Claudio's gullible, overly trusting nature would naturally lead him to believe not only what he was told but also what he thought he'd actually witnessed. Moreover, the fact that his mentor, the Prince, was also taken in makes the fraud seem even more plausible.

Finally, just to prove how many strings he has to his bow, Shakespeare invents two more twin eavesdropping scenes. In the first, Benedict is persuaded of Beatrice's love for him, and then she is persuaded of his love for her. Benedict and Beatrice, like others in this play, are eavesdroppers duped through their own eavesdropping, for their eavesdropping naturally leads them to believe what they hear is the truth.

Yet these paired comic scenes are not, as we have seen, exactly carbon copies of each other. Although the Benedict and Beatrice episodes have the same effect on both eavesdroppers, the action unfolds in entirely different ways. Benedict, more sensitive of this public image, takes almost twice as long to be conned by the prose of the Prince, Leonato, and Claudio as Beatrice does by the verse of Ursula and Hero.

To sum up all the examples in this work, Shakespeare includes six eavesdropping episodes in *Much Ado About Nothing*, each with differing qualities: three are staged and three are reported; in three examples the eavesdropper is deceived intentionally and in two the eavesdropper is deceived unintentionally; in three examples eavesdropping is used for positive purposes, and in two for malicious purposes.

With this survey of eavesdropping one might well have thought that every possible combination has now been exploited. But Shakespeare must have so appreciated the potential for effective drama in this device that he continued to evolve new variations. For example, an entirely new theatrical experience occurs when the presence of the eavesdropper is suspected. As a case in point, in *Hamlet,* the Prince might well suppose others are listening to his conversation with Ophelia. After all, Polonius has tried to test Hamlet's mental state, and that interview was immediately followed by a discussion between the Prince and Rosencrantz and Guildenstern in which Hamlet learns that his school friends were called to Denmark to help the King and Queen find out the reasons for his troubling behavior.

So when Hamlet comes upon Ophelia praying and finds she also just happens to be holding gifts from him that she wishes to return, he might well be suspicious. Moreover, something in her manner, or moved by his own doubts of her honesty, prompts Hamlet to ask an unexpected question, one that seems remote from his pronouncements on women and marriage. To throw her off guard, he suddenly asks her, "Where's your father?" And that query leads him to pronounce his threat: "Those that are married already—all but one—shall live." If Claudius is not present to hear them for himself, Hamlet can fully expect these words will be reported to his uncle.

In this instance, then, Shakespeare presents an eavesdropping attempt that is both ambiguous and revealing: is Hamlet reacting to his own suspicion that he is being spied upon, or is his fury entirely the manifestation of his feelings toward his mother and uncle, or is his behavior quite possibly the consequence of some combination of these? In addition to our fascination with the complex motives for his words and actions, we are also prompted to wonder whether Hamlet has quite cleverly put his uncle on guard in order to make him show his hand more readily, or whether the Prince, revealing a potential weakness in his own nature, manifests a loss of self-control that will soon lead him to kill the wrong man.

The issue of self-control is, of course, a basic one in this play and crucial for the tragic hero in the eavesdropping episode in his mother's chamber. Here Shakespeare dramatizes how dangerous, indeed deadly, a business eavesdropping can be. Distressed by Gertrude's calls for help, Polonius echoes them from his hiding place behind the tapestry in her bedroom. Hamlet stabs through the fabric thinking that he has killed the king but instead commits "a rash and bloody deed." Now, like his uncle, he is a murderer: eavesdropping can be played for more than comic intrigue.

In his exploration of its more serious possibilities, Shakespeare demonstrates the intensely dramatic potential of eavesdropping episodes in two plays that followed. Near the conclusion of *Troilus and Cressida* we have a new twist on the *Love's Labour's Lost* sonnet-reading sequence in which the young men listen secretly to each other confessing their love. In *Troilus and Cressida* one eavesdropper observes others deliberately eavesdropping, but rather than a shared response, as in *Love's Labour's Lost,* those involved in this late play express entirely different reactions and emotions.

Ulysses leads Troilus to where he can see and hear Diomedes flirt with Cressida. At the same time, the four of them are watched by that bitter commentator, Thersites. The young Troilus is anguished to see Cressida flirt with Diomedes and reluctantly give him the token Troilus had earlier given her. Although he did "swear patience," Troilus, in his anger and disillusion, can hardly contain himself from being heard by those he observes, and Ulysses, fearful of being discovered, encourages Troilus to leave. Meanwhile, the four involved in this action are themselves the subject of Thersites's remarks, who finds in this incident a proof of his view of life that all's "Lechery, lechery, still wars and lechery! Nothing else holds fashion. A burning devil take them!"

The dramatic interest here is in the tension generated by the very different emotions displayed by the characters: Cressida's divided self, attracted to Diomedes but yet reluctant to betray Troilus; Diomedes, blunt in his sexual advances and unwilling to allow Cressida to tease him; Ulysses, concerned by the devastating effect what they witness has on Troilus and worried that the Greeks will discover them; Troilus, distraught, for he can neither deny nor believe what he sees; and, finally, Thersites, who takes all of this as a validation of his low estimate of human nature. This is indeed a highly sophisticated eavesdropping scene used for complex purposes both of character revelation and plot development.

As a final example that demonstrates Shakespeare's continued experimentation with the theatrical possibilities of eavesdropping, we can consider the scene late in *Othello* when Iago stations the hero where he can secretly observe a conversation between Iago and Cassio. Shakespeare seems to be particularly interested in using this episode as a way of dramatizing the hero's state of mind. His frenzied mental condition is manifested by making him an eavesdropper on a conversation that he does not quite hear.

In *Othello*, the situation is somewhat similar to what Shakespeare put on stage in the paired Benedict and Beatrice scenes in *Much Ado About Nothing*: eavesdroppers can be easily duped because like all of us they take for truth what they wish to believe or expect to hear. But in *Othello*, Shakespeare made the incident far more psychologically astute because in this case the conversation the audience hears is not the same as what the eavesdropper invents. Since he is at too remote a distance to catch the actual words of Cassio and Iago, Othello simply makes up the dialogue between the two men, imagining what he expects to be spoken and interpreting the gestures he sees in a manner that supports his expectations. This scene is especially painful because Othello wrongly believes he is hearing what, in fact, he dreads to hear.

Yet Othello is so absolutely certain of what was said that he later tells Desdemona, Cassio "confessed . . . That he hath . . . used thee." In this example, we have a character believing he heard what he most feared because he was psychologically primed to expect it. Shakespeare is dramatizing how we accept as true not what is established by logical proof or fact but rather what our mind believes the truth to be. Reality is as the individual psyche interprets it. Malvolio, the butt of eavesdroppers, can be false-persuaded of Olivia's love, and Othello, himself an eavesdropper, can become convinced of Desdemona's dishonor.

The number of times that eavesdropping scenes occur in his plays is an indication of how highly Shakespeare valued them. Indeed,

for a playwright such scenes can accomplish much: they place the
audience in a position of superior knowledge, thereby opening
possibilities for dramatic irony; they enable the playwright to dramatize a character's evolving state of mind in a way that is far more
dramatic than the soliloquy; they are eminently actable, for they
make use of the various playing-areas of the stage; they can generate a wide variety of audience responses—from laughter and pathos
to surprise and horror. And finally, a writer can show off his skill
in playwrighting by staging eavesdropping scenes in a variety of
ways: performed and reported; unintentional and deliberate; single
instances or multiple; for positive or malicious ends; in prose or
verse; in brief or at length; for purposes of character, or plot development, or both. Simply put, the extraordinary range and variety of examples in the Shakespeare canon are evidence of genius
at work.

The play-within-a-play is one of Shakespeare's favorite theatrical
devices.[35] The elaborate practical joke played on Christopher Sly in
the prologue to *The Taming of the Shrew* effectively turns the
whole shrew-taming story into a play-within-a-play. On the other
hand, in *Henry IV, Part One,* when Hal and Falstaff take turns at
impersonating Bolingbroke and acting out Hal's part in his forthcoming interview with his father, a brief and rather rudimentary
play-within-the-play is performed. And at other times separate entertainments with their own story line become a way of embellish-
ing the larger work. *A Midsummer Night's Dream* and *Love's
Labour's Lost* both include examples of independent playlets or in-
terludes integrated into the main action. In the former, the Athenian workmen present the "tedious brief scene of young Pyramus/
And his love Thisbe, very tragical mirth." This hilarious spoof of
a tale of confused and mistaken lovers naturally recalls the comic
mishaps of the two young couples in the main action of the plot.
But since dreaming and playacting are, after all, of a similar, unreal
nature, the rather harsh, unsympathetic reception Bottom and his
fellows receive from the young people suggests that they are unaware or deny their own recent history. They have forgotten how
difficult it is to separate asleep from awake, the make-believe from

the real, although only a few scenes earlier one of them had acknowledged the difficulty:

> Are you sure
> That we are awake? It seems to me
> That yet we sleep, we dream.

> (IV.i)

If the "Pyramus and Thisby" interlude is merely a misguided
effort to "beguile/ The lazy time" perhaps one might say that of
Shakespeare's play, too. Surely in that case one should remember
the advice of Theseus on playgoing and behave accordingly: "the
best in this kind are but shadows; and the worst no worse, if imagination amend them." (V.i) For ultimately, as Theseus points out,
the audience also is to be judged, and the criterion for judging them
is the way they respond to the actors. As he says: "the kinder we,
to give them thanks for nothing." Might there be a bit of personal
bias on the part of the playwright expressed in this notion?

Love's Labour's Lost also incorporates a low-comedy pageant or
play-within-a-play in its last act. The subject of this entertainment,
we may recall, is the Nine Worthies, such men as Hercules, Hector,
Pompey, and Alexander. As was the case in *A Midsummer Night's
Dream*, the interlude reflects the theme of the play as a whole,
which is to question the price paid in the pursuit of fame. And as
in *A Midsummer Night's Dream*, the performance is continually
disrupted by the comments of the spectators and the incompetence
of the players, so that scarcely a full speech gets spoken. Laughter
is rather the end result, though indirectly the subject matter here
raises the point that the effort involved in holding on to "the bubble reputation" can result in a life that is diminished, denied the
pleasures that come from such mundane pursuits as love, friendship, and sociability—"where I well may dine . . . [or] where to
meet some mistress fine." (I.i) And all the puns, jokes, wit-com-
bats, and games that occur throughout—the masquerades and
masques, songs and dances, pageants and competitions—are finally
combined at the close into a celebration and appreciation of our
time-bound existence. Every human life should be treated with

dignity, wisdom even Don Armado knows: "Sweet chucks, beat not the bones of the buried. When he breathed, he was a man." With sound reason, some argue that this is Shakespeare's most sophisticated, complex, demanding, and rewarding comedy.

The incorporation of a play-within-a-play in *Hamlet* is very different from these earlier examples, although like them this one is also written in a poetic style that distinguishes it from the usual dialogue of the play as a whole. In this tragedy, the entertainment staged for the court of Denmark is intended by the hero to prove Claudius has murdered his brother, since, as Hamlet knows,

> guilty creatures sitting at a play
> Have, by the very cunning of the scene,
> Been struck so to the soul that presently
> They have proclaim'd their malefactions.
>
> (II.ii)

Hamlet arranges for the acting company visiting Elsinore to perform a work in their repertory in which "one scene . . . comes near the circumstance/ . . . of my father's death." He will then be able to determine his uncle's innocence or guilt by Claudius's reaction.

Immediately before the troupe of players actually speak their lines, however, they perform a dumb show, a mime, that in this instance replicates the events that will occur in the spoken performance. Here this theatrical embellishment prepares the playhouse audience for what will follow; surprisingly, Claudius seems unaffected by what he sees or is not watching when poison is poured into the sleeping player–king's ears and the poisoner woos the recently widowed player–queen.

The dumb show is followed immediately by the enacting of the text. When the villain of this play-within-a-play makes his entrance, Hamlet identifies him as "one Lucianus, nephew to the King." Since the plot is intended to reenact the version of the fratricide told to Hamlet by his father's ghost, Shakespeare should cast Lucianus as the king's brother. Turning him into a nephew is an unexpected and intriguing alteration, for it makes the poisoner Lucianus metaphorically both Claudius and Hamlet. The change suggests not only that Hamlet, knowing the truth of what his uncle has done, is a threat to Claudius but also that Lucianus prefigures Hamlet's role as both murderer and revenger.

Perhaps, had Hamlet named Lucianus the brother of the sleeping king, Claudius might then have put a stop to the performance and his guilty conscience would never have been discovered. Or perhaps, by calling the character of the villain "nephew" to the king, Hamlet hopes to increase Claudius's sense of uneasiness so that he is less in control of his emotions, unable to prevent himself from reacting when he hears "the talk of the poisoning." Of course, Shakespeare's tragedy never makes entirely clear what Claudius is thinking or how he should behave in this scene until Ophelia sees him rise, and he shouts, "Give o'er the play."

In any case, the dumb show and the play-within-a-play, occurring in the middle of the third act, form the pivotal scene of the tragedy, for they establish the truth of the ghost's words and open the way for the remainder of the action. From this point on, the conflict between nephew and uncle is explicit: Hamlet has confirmation of his uncle's guilt, and Claudius knows it. The stage device of the play-within-the-play, which had served earlier as a delightful comic diversion and variation, has now become a crucial element in the design of the whole tragedy. Here it shifts the action from the issue of establishing whether Claudius is guilty to the question of how Hamlet will pursue his revenge. In this instance, the play-within-the-play is essential not only in the development of the plot but also in redefining and clarifying the nature and relationships of the major characters in the story.

No other dumb show or play-within-a-play in all of Shakespeare's works is as complex or crucial as this one, which Hamlet calls, appropriately enough, "The Mousetrap." But Shakespeare is not above using theatrical devices such as the dumb show simply to add dash and color, a bit of spectacle to the entertainment. In *Pericles*, for example, dumb shows are performed in Acts II, III, and IV. In addition, in the second act of this play six knights silently march across the stage on their way to a tournament. As each appears, he is identified, and the device on his shield is described. To add a bit of pageantry, processions of this sort might also be expected to occur in the staging of funerals, coronations, or battle scenes; *Richard III* offers occasions when the plot calls for all three. In the second scene of *Troilus and Cressida,* Shakespeare manages to use the appearance of the Trojan warriors who file across the stage returning from battle as an opportunity to identify each. Pandarus says to his niece, Cressida: "I'll tell you them all by their names as they pass by." Here the spectacle of the actors crossing the stage becomes an opportunity for presenting expository material.

Surely among the most delightful and inventive of Shakespeare's theatrical embellishments is his use of music, both vocal and instrumental. The plays include some one hundred songs, and their stage directions frequently call for the sounds of specific musical instruments. Actually, in Shakespeare's day, music was expected in the theater as part of the entertainment, before, during, or after the performance of a play, and all acting companies included singers and professional musicians.

Music was highly regarded by this audience, for harmonious sounds were thought a reflection of cosmic perfection. And by analogy, the orderliness of the universe, expressed in terms that have musical references, can also describe the best qualities of human conduct: "good time," "measure," "concord," "unison." In addition to the positive effects of hearing the sounds of pleasant music, graceful dancing was regarded as the physical representation of this harmony. *As You Like It* and *Much Ado About Nothing* both conclude with dances, for they are a fitting ending for such joyous comedies, celebrating the marital and political happiness achieved.

Instrumental music could also carry symbolic meaning for the audience in Shakespeare's playhouse. For example, the sound of cornets and trumpets signified the presence of the court; oboes (or "hautboys," which were louder and harsher than their modern counterparts) accompanied supernatural spirits from hell or presaged murder. The spectator at the Globe would have thought it ominous that oboes, not trumpets, provided the stage music as

King Duncan arrives at Macbeth's castle where he will be murdered that night.

When he arrives, the King's remarks—"This castle hath a pleasant seat. The air/ Nimbly and sweetly recommends itself/Unto our senses"—are full of irony after the sinister music that has just preceded them. Oboes convey the same meaning in *Titus Andronicus* just before Titus appears dressed as a cook, serving pies with the children of one of his guests baked inside, and in *Antony and Cleopatra,* oboe music is heard ominously from beneath the stage to foretell that "the god Hercules whom Antony loved/ Now leaves him."

In contrast, string music is never threatening. It often foreshadows a happy event or accompanies a positive change, from hate to love, from suspicion to trust, from vengeance to forgiveness, even from death to life. Sweet music is played to restore King Lear to his sanity. And in *The Winter's Tale* Paulina orders sweet music, probably the sound of viols, as the statue of Hermione is unveiled and returns to life. Again, in *Pericles,* the doctor, Cerimon, calls for music to revive the supposedly dead Thaisa: "The viol once more. How thou stirr'st, thou block!/ The music there! I pray you give her air./ Gentlemen, this queen will live." His cure is not so improbable as it may seem, for to some Renaissance thinkers the rhythmic contractions of the human heart could be made to respond to the alternating upbeat and downbeat in music rhythm. The notion is similar to the phenomenon of sympathetic vibration by which the plucking of one string can make a nearby second one vibrate with it, if the two are perfectly attuned. So sounding strongly rhythmic music with a tempo approximating the pulse beat of the human heart could cause a stilled heart to beat again. To the music of the viol, Thaisa reawakens to life.

Instrumental music, with its ability to affect mankind's physical, mental, and spiritual state, was clearly regarded as a force of great power: according to Lorenzo in *The Merchant of Venice*, there is "naught so stockish, hard, and full of rage/ But music for the time doth change his nature." Yet vocal music holds an even higher place. As a kind of rational music, enriched by language and the sound of the human voice, with the lyrics matching the line of the melody, it is music in its most perfect form.

Shakespeare makes use of three types of vocal music to further the plot or develop the characters. The simplest is the use of folksongs or popular balladlike ditties, with words and music presumably well known to his audience. These are performed spontaneously by an actor without accompaniment. When the sailor Stephano in *The Tempest* swears to swallow no water until his keg of wine is empty, he celebrates his resolve with a good drinking song:

> The master, the swabber, the boatswain, and I
> The gunner, and his mate,
> Loved Mall, Meg, Marian, and Margery,
> But none of us cared for Kate.
>
> (II.ii)

This rendering of a popular ballad is a form of character music, directly conveying the personality of the singer.

Another amusing use of this type of song occurs in *Twelfth Night*, where it contributes both to character development and plot. Drunk and boisterous, Sir Toby Belch and Sir Andrew Aguecheek, along with the clown Feste, delight in their "catch" or "round," a vocal game like "Three Blind Mice." Since the noise of their late night carousing disturbs the humorless Malvolio, and since a catch has no ending except for the exhaustion of the singers, the refrain becomes the perfect response to the outraged steward. They will not hold their peace, even as they sing "Hold thy peace," and even as Malvolio bids them to do just that.

In *Othello,* Shakespeare uses the popular ballad in a more subtle manner to dramatize how clever and devious is the villain Iago. He rouses his listeners to raise their cups in a drinking song:

> And let me the cannikin clink, clink;
> And let me the cannikin clink.
> A soldier's a man;
> A life's but a span,
> Why then, let a soldier drink.
>
> (II.iii)

Here he seems to be a warm, sociable fellow soldier, but the character he impersonates through the music is assumed rather than genuine. In fact, this devilish schemer is out to get Cassio drunk as part of a plan to cause trouble for Othello. Like Shylock and Shakespeare's other villains, Iago has no true ear for music.

A second category of song in Shakespeare's works is one that adapts popular music to fit a specific dramatic context. Words and melody, presumably well known to the audience, are modified to suit the play's character and situation. In this way, the state of mind of the singer can be conveyed by the changes the playwright has made in the original lyrics. These songs also would be performed without accompaniment.

Ophelia's mad scene in *Hamlet* is a notable example of this use of music. Indeed, the fact that she sings before the king and queen in so informal a manner is itself indicative of her derangement, for her conduct is inappropriate. Moreover, the pathos of her situation, the helplessness she feels, her sense of isolation and rejection would be movingly conveyed by the thin, wavering voice of the boy actor who wanders distractedly on stage singing snatches of old songs.

The lyrics to the music convey her feelings about her father's death and Hamlet's behavior toward her. In the original version, the words to her dirge, "He is dead and gone," are: "Which bewept to the grave did go." But Ophelia sings, "Which bewept to the grave did not go." Although this change contradicts the sense of the stanza and breaks the meter, it indicates how deeply she is affected by the hasty and unceremonious burial of her father. Her other lyrics, "For bonny sweet Robin is all my joy" and the four stanzas of a St. Valentine's Day song, reveal her concern with courtship, romance, and especially premarital love. All of this involves Hamlet: fear that he has rejected her; anxiety that he has gone mad; horror that he has murdered her father; and distress that she has (or has not) remained chaste.

Another equally effective example of this use of such emotionally charged music is Shakespeare's adaptation of the "Willow Song" in *Othello*, which was originally sung by a man recounting his sudden rejection by the woman he loved. Desdemona's first stanza follows the popular lyric closely, only making the necessary change in the sex of the singer. But as the song proceeds, Shakespeare makes additional alterations.

Desdemona is in great emotional turmoil. She has just been reviled and cursed by her husband, yet she can find no explanation for his exceptionally cruel and harsh treatment of her. As she prepares for bed, this song comes into her mind because in her distress she recalls her mother's maid:

> She was in love; and he she loved proved mad
> And did forsake her. She had a song of 'Willow';
> An old thing 'twas, but it expressed her fortune.
> And she died singing it.

> (IV.iii)

With the sex of this singer changed, the old song is now appropriate for Desdemona as well as her mother's maid. The simplicity of the melody, the false start—"Nay, that's not next," she says as she tries to remember the sequence of the verses—all help convey her fear and sense of rejection and abandonment.

Her last stanza, as Shakespeare has recast it, differs considerably from the original. According to the popular version the words are: "Come all you forsaken, and mourn you with me/ Who speaks of a false love, none's falser than she." But in place of this, Desdemona sings: "I called my love false love; but what said he then?/ If I court moe women, you'll couch with moe men." Shakespeare's alteration, from the original lover's complaint that his sweetheart will be false to Desdemona's awareness that she will be blamed for being false, reinforces Othello's earlier accusations of promiscuity. The last of these allegations is, in fact, repeated a final time just before Othello strangles her: "she must die, else she'll betray more men."

Although the dramatic effectiveness of the song is enhanced by knowing the model on which it is based, one need not be familiar with the original to be moved by this version. Shakespeare has prepared the moment: the simple pathos of the melody, the anguish of the singer, the tension in the audience knowing that Othello has vowed his wife will die that night, all contribute to make this one of the most painful moments in the play.

Finally, what is perhaps the most interesting and powerful use of music occurs when original pieces, composed for a specific moment in a play, are presented by a professional singer. The lyrics of this type of song usually have more complexity and finesse than those of the popular ballads, and, unlike the singing of Iago, Ophelia, or Desdemona, these art songs as a rule require musical accompaniment. The dialogue that precedes their performance very often incorporates references to the necessary preparations or to the instruments required. In some cases the arrangements were composed by distinguished musicians: Thomas Morley wrote the music for "It Was A Lover and His Lass" in *As You Like It;* and the lutanist Robert Johnson composed the melodies for two of Ariel's songs in *The Tempest.*

In *Twelfth Night*, Feste twice matches his song to the personality and the mood of his listener or to the action of the play. For Duke Orsino, full of self-indulgent melancholy and not a little enjoying his role as the languishing lover, Feste sings the mournful dirge, "Come away, come away, death," with its complaint: "I am slain by a fair cruel maid." Whether Shakespeare fitted his words to Thomas Morley's melody or the two collaborated is unclear, but however the words and music came together, the song, "O Mistress mine, where are you roaming?," suits the moment in the play when it is sung. For the Lady Olivia, mistress of this household, who has continually rejected the Duke's suit, has now fallen in love with his page, the boyish Viola disguised as a young man.

At the close of the play, after all the action is over, Feste comes out on stage alone to sing a little ballad about life, love, sex, and marriage, a song that Shakespeare includes again in *King Lear.* Despite the generally happy ending of *Twelfth Night,* the refrain of Feste's lyrics reminds his audience that "the rain it raineth every day." Joy is never unalloyed; happiness is a sometime-thing. The song brings once again to the forefront the overall tone of this work. *Twelfth Night* is not a comedy of pure delight, but of pleasure moderated by a trace of melancholy caused by an awareness of the vicissitudes of time and the weaknesses of humanity. "Knaves and thieves," "swaggering," and "tosspots" are recounted in the lyrics as the singer progresses from child to adult, from youth to age.

The two splendid songs that end *Love's Labour's Lost* serve to sum up the action, comment on the meaning of the play, and establish a closing mood. Immediately before they are performed, Costard, the clown, reveals that the country wench, Jaquenetta, is pregnant. Then a messenger, dressed in black, unexpectedly arrives from the French court to announce the death of the king. News of new life and recent death occur almost at the same time, and under the pressure of events at home, the Princess of France must leave immediately. The extravagant ambitions of the young men and their courtship games now seem remote from the real concerns of existence, and the exigencies of the moment are, in the words of the French princess, too demanding "to make a world-without-end bargain in." Vows of eternal love and devotion cannot be properly exchanged or accepted "at the latest minute of the hour." As the ladies take their final leave and the young men have agreed to undergo proofs of their love, the songs of Winter and Spring, of the owl and the cuckoo, are performed.

Supposedly a remnant from the hilarious pageant of the Worthies and coming after the absurdities and exaggerations of the young lords, the two songs close the play by reasserting the joys and imperatives of everyday existence. The "when" and "then" that are repeated in each of the stanzas emphasize the stability of nature even with its recurring changes, and their subject matter focuses attentively on the details of daily life, its pleasures, fears, pains, and labors:

> When icicles hang by the wall,
>   And Dick the shepherd blows his nail,
> And Tom bears logs into the hall,
>   And milk comes frozen home in pail,
> When blood is nipped, and ways be foul,
> Then nightly sings the staring owl . . .

(V.ii)

Moreover, in their language, meter, and rhyme the two songs demonstrate a deceptive naïveté, a seeming simplicity that can only be accomplished by deliberate artfulness. The "taffeta phrases, silken terms precise,/ Three-piled hyperboles, [and] spruce affection" of the men have given way at last to "honest plain words" that are both more moving and persuasive. The songs of spring and winter are proof of what music, poetry, and language can achieve in perfect combination.

In at least two instances, songs provide an indirect way of commenting on the action that encourages the viewer to reevaluate what is said and done. In *The Merchant of Venice*, Portia hopes that Bassanio will make the right choice, the casket made of lead, so they can marry. She orders a song to be sung while he is making his decision, and the lyrics begin by rhyming "bred" with "head." Is this an appeal to his unconscious, prompting him to reject gold and silver in favor of the baser metal? Such a possibility is not out of character for this heroine. Though she has sworn to abide by her father's will, which directs that her husband will be determined through the casket-test, Portia has admitted that she is not above tinkering with the way the test is administered. For example, if her heavy-drinking, German suitor decides to face the challenge, she plans to "set a deep glass of Rhenish wine on the contrary casket, for . . . I know that he will choose it. I will do anything . . . ere I will be married to a sponge." Portia's ultra-cleverness, her willingness to tinker with the rules in a shady way, are qualities in her nature that will be demonstrated again by her behavior in the trial against Shylock.

In *As You Like It*, the play with the most vocal music, we also hear a song offering another perspective on the action that has immediately preceded it. In this scene, the kind-hearted and sentimental Duke Senior is sympathetic to the misfortunes of the hero, Orlando, and his faithful old servant, Adam, who is resting off stage, too weak with age and hunger to travel further. While Orlando leaves in order to carry Adam to the Duke's table for food and comfort, Jaques delivers his cynical summation on the course of human existence. Our lives, he observes, pass through seven ages that end only in "second childishness and mere oblivion/ Sans teeth, sans eyes, sans taste, sans everything."

As soon as Jaques has finished his "strange eventful history," Orlando enters with his "venerable burden." And while the two exhausted travelers dine, we hear the song "Blow, blow thou winter wynde/ Thou art not so unkind/ As man's ingratitude." The care and solicitude that Orlando, the Duke, and his men show for Adam are proof that Jaques's jaundiced view of life is only partial and biased, for old age is not, as he says, "mere oblivion" "sans everything." The treatment accorded Adam is marked by its dignity and respect, concern and humanity. In the words of the song, "Most friendship is feigning, most loving mere folly," but that does not mean all friendship and all loving are without merit. To think so is to hold an extreme, incorrect, and ultra-negative view of life— exactly Jaques's situation.

The words and music of the song enable Shakespeare to dramatize another perspective on the action. The singer, standing apart, can offer a judgment that avoids a didactic or moralistic interpretation. Such a song as this, although removed from the drama since it does not advance the story, nevertheless offers a means of integrating the action, of manipulating the various points of view until cynicism and sentimentality, reserved judgment and loving-kindness have been molded into a wise and comprehensive view of life. Clearly, Shakespeare found music, both instrumental and vocal, a highly adaptable and flexible means of enriching his plays, offering relief from the spoken word and novelty to the wearying ear.

And to celebrate the high spirits and reconciliation that mark the world of the play, *As You Like It* concludes with both music and dancing, as the festivities of the multiple weddings are overseen by Hymen, the god of marriage.

Perhaps the most complex and extravagant example of theatrical embellishment in Shakespearean drama is his incorporation of elements of the masque. This was the most lavish form of entertainment at the court of Elizabeth's successor, James I, and it was the type of spectacle most preferred by James's consort, Queen Anne. These Jacobean extravaganzas were performed by professional

actors and singers who were joined by members of the aristocracy
and even of the royal family. The text, usually a kind of mythic or
symbolic story combining verse, song, and dance, was presented
with elaborate and carefully designed costumes and scenery before
a select audience. A special characteristic of some of these scripts is
their inclusion of an anti-masque, a grotesque, dissonant, or negative image of life that serves as contrast to the glories manifested by
the rule of King James. Elements of these exclusive theatricals
found their way into the public theater. And younger playwrights
in their tragicomedies incorporated some of these new, special effects in their work. So Shakespeare, especially in his late plays, may
be responding to as well as developing theatrical innovations to
please an evolving fashion.

Music and dancing—the stage directions call for "twelve sa-
tyrs"—are a part of the stage activity that makes the sheep-shearing
festival in *The Winter's Tale* so colorful. In *The Tempest*, Prospero,
the wonder-working magician, stages a wedding masque to celebrate the nuptials of his daughter, feeling that he must "bestow
upon the eyes of this young couple/ Some vanity of mine art." The
goddesses Iris and Ceres appear, and joined by Juno, the Queen of
the Gods, they "bless this twain, that they may prosperous be/
And honored in their issue." Then the three women call forth
Nymphs who join with Reapers "in a graceful dance."

Suddenly, Prospero causes this magic spectacle to vanish; it dissolves, "melted into thin air," and this "insubstantial pageant" is
followed by something resembling an anti-masque. The evil plotting comic characters, Stephano and Trinculo, led by the savage
Caliban, enter bedraggled and at last are chased offstage by "spirits
in the shape of dogs and hounds."

Masque elements are also included in two plays Shakespeare
wrote toward the end of his career with his collaborator, John
Fletcher. The dancing spirits in *Henry VIII*, who appeared to a
sleeping Queen Katherine, described earlier in this chapter, are
surely masque-like, and *Two Noble Kinsmen* borrows an anti-
masque that actually appeared first in an entertainment by the
playwright Francis Beaumont. Such theatrical embellishments of
the drama, combining music, costume, dance, and song, can add

variety to the dialogue and dazzle the eyes of the spectators with their color and movement. And when such masque-like spectacles are well integrated into the story, as in *The Winter's Tale* and *The Tempest*, they enrich and extend the narrative flow of the plot.

This overview of examples demonstrates how Shakespeare prefers to rework the usual theatrical devices of the contemporary theater in order to put a new twist on traditional elements—an eavesdropper imagines what he most fears to hear, or a song's lyrics can be made to comment ironically, or pathetically, or touchingly on the plot situation. The creative impulse drives the dramatist to attempt different, ingenious, and novel ways of using stage elements, ways that will both advance and enrich his play as well as delight and surprise his spectators.

8

Resolving the Action

" "The good ended happily, and the bad unhappily. That is what fiction means." This definition of the fate of characters in literature, rigidly held by the governess Miss Prism in Oscar Wilde's *The Importance of Being Earnest*, is amusing because it is both absolute and all-inclusive. It suggests that fiction is written only to provide a simple morality that is seldom, if ever, found in real life. Yet Miss Prism's axiom reveals not only that her literary judgment is limited but also that she does not know her Shakespeare.

Often, in fact, the concluding action of a Shakespeare play does not present a world order that is quite as neat as what Miss Prism expects. In some cases the audience is actually unsure of how to interpret the ending. Even when all loose ends seem neatly tied, ambiguous possibilities are deliberately encouraged. For example, for those who are sensitive to what is really going on the final speech may be presented as kind of a play-within-a-play, and so meant to be understood simply as a pretense, a make-believe. Or the resolution may be deferred, unstaged and postponed to a time beyond the compass of what can be acted. Or the ending may simply bring us back to where we started: although principles have been debated, wars have been fought, and people have died, the final moments return us to exactly the situation that existed at the opening of the action. In other cases, the resolution is bitterly ironic, matters having turned out in ways quite contrary to the intentions of those who hoped to control the course of events. Or the serious action of the plot may be undercut by the comic scenes so that lofty ideals and high principles are shown to be inseparable from, if not an integral part, of political maneuvering and self-interest. In still other instances, the ending is left completely open and unresolved: the decisive step is never taken.

Yet perhaps Miss Prism can take some comfort from the fact that even so intelligent a reader and so great a lover of Shakespeare as Dr. Johnson criticized the playwright, for "he seems to write without any moral purpose" and "makes no just distribution of good or evil." In the final analysis, Shakespeare's plays must reflect his realization that life cannot be reduced to a simple formula and that his dramas must do far more than show us good rewarded and evil punished.

In the last scene of *The Taming of the Shrew*, the three newly married men in the story agree to a contest to prove which of them has the "most obedient" wife. Her rivals fail; yet Katherine displays an extraordinary deference, humility, and submissiveness to her new husband's will despite her reputation for independence and bad temper. It all looks genuine enough, but Katherine may indeed have come to a new understanding of how to find happiness in Petruchio's high-spirited and whimsically humorous behavior. She must be aware that the husbands have some private game afoot when the three women are summoned. So her performance in abject accordance with Petruchio's requests may be seen as rather a version of the Christopher Sly play-within-a-play that began this drama. Those in the audience along with Petruchio may be witnessing a bit of pretending, convincing enough to win him the prize money for having the most obedient spouse. And as was shown in the Christopher Sly practical joke that opened the play, behavior changes to suit the role assumed. For Petruchio has taught Katherine to enjoy the game, to take delight in returning the serve, to relish the pleasure that comes from a shared sense of humor. Their mutual taste for quick-witted inventiveness, previously dramatized, shows how well suited they are as marriage partners, and how these rather complex characters have come to an affectionate understanding and appreciation of each other's nature. Such a marriage of true minds is characteristic of Shakespeare's mature lovers.

The preparation for this moment is key to a proper response. The entente cordiale worked out by Katherine and Petruchio and the conversation among the three couples immediately before the contest might well lead us to suspect that the bit of pretense in the final moments is related to the opening Christopher Sly gambit. Things are not always, if ever, exactly what they seem, Shakespeare suggests. The relationship of Katherine and Petruchio is a good deal more spirited than she admits when she tells the other wives: "Thy husband is thy lord, thy life, thy keeper,/ Thy head, thy sovereign."

Moreover, the boy playing the role of Katherine is rather like the disguised young Page who appears with Sly and claims to be "your wife in all obedience." Indeed, women can prove to be far more clever and subtle creatures than some men may realize. Katherine grants that men are far stronger, but never that they are wiser. Since performance as well as language guide our response to what takes place on stage, the opening and closing of this play may well be related in theme.

Katherine's critical speech on the role of wives leaves the interpretation of *The Taming of the Shrew* open and suggestive. By contrast, there is nothing indeterminate about the ending of *Love's Labour's Lost*, though even the characters on stage acknowledge its unconventionality. Before the four women will accept the marriage proposals offered in the last scene, the four young men, who have broken their oath to fast, study, and live apart, will have to wait a year, fulfilling the injunctions of their mistresses. Only in this way can the King of Navarre and his friends prove that their devotion is genuine. As Berowne, the spokesman for the group, points out, "Our wooing doth not end like an old play;/ Jack hath not Jill." And since a year must elapse before they can marry, he adds, "That's too long for a play."

So with marriages delayed, Shakespeare returns *Love's Labour's Lost* to the interrupted masque of the "Worthies" in the final moments of the play. Closing with the songs of the owl and the cuckoo, of winter and spring, the music achieves far more than the usual comic ending. The beauty of the songs and the sweet sadness of the close more than compensate for postponing what we have come to expect, and, of course, this substitution of song in place of wedding festivities makes for a poignant and unforgettable moment.[36]

As a general principle, the greater the number of celebrants at the end of a comedy, the more joyous it is. But Shakespeare does not believe all can be made happy. In his view, happiness, unlike sunshine, does not fall on all alike. Someone at the end of a Shakespearean play is often left out, excluded either voluntarily or involuntarily, from the renewed, healthy society that is celebrated at the close. Marriage and reconciliation are not for all; isolation, rejection, and discontent are for some their undiluted portion.

Perhaps it is his heritage as a Vice figure, an Iago-like character who is evil simply by definition, that makes Don John in *Much Ado About Nothing* so malicious:

> it must not be denied but I am a plain-dealing villain. . . . If I had my mouth, I would bite; if I had my liberty, I would do my liking.
>
> (I.iii)

And so in the end, as we might expect, this cruel slanderer remains unconverted. The last we hear of him is that he has been caught and "brought with armed men to Messina" where he will have to answer for his crimes. In the meantime, the best that can be done is to resume the dancing, to continue the party that celebrates the two marriages completed despite all of Don John's efforts. As Benedict says in the closing words of the play: "Think not of him till tomorrow. I'll devise thee brave punishments for him. Strike up, pipers!"

The villain Don John is constitutionally unable to find pleasure in the happiness of others, deriving satisfaction only from his success at causing them pain. Naturally, he has no place in the joyous ending. But in the world of *As You Like It* even the villainous brothers, Duke Frederick and Oliver, are metamorphosed once they enter the forest. Duke Senior's sibling, Frederick, who came to Arden "purposely to take/ His brother here and put him to the sword," has been instantly transformed by the air of the pastoral:

> And to the skirts of this wild wood he came,
> Where, meeting with an old religious man,
> After some questions with him, was converted
> Both from his enterprise and from the world.
>
> (V.iv)

Frederick has conveniently chosen to retire, hermit-like, from the world, returning the ducal crown and the lands he usurped. And Oliver, who earlier threatened Orlando's life—"my soul, yet I know not why, hates nothing more than he"—is also altered by his experience in the forest:

> I do not shame
> To tell you what I was, since my conversion
> So sweetly tastes, being the thing I am.
>
> (IV.iii)

Obviously, such sudden and unexpected changes of character must be accepted as conventional elements in ancient tales and pastoral fantasies.

Only Jaques remains apart. Yet he is not a villain, like Don John, or even of a sometime-villainous nature, like Frederick or Oliver. Jaques may have been a libertine, but he was never malicious. Instead, he is one who is happy in his own unhappiness, finding pleasure in his own particular melancholy. "I do love it better than laughing," he admits to Rosalind. And so, Jaques excludes himself from the party: "I am for other than for dancing measures," he explains. Even in such a storybook world, Shakespeare's view of humankind clearly takes in many different specimens and many different psychological complexities. "O, the difference of man and man," as Goneril observes in *King Lear*.

With *Much Ado About Nothing* and *As You Like It*, *Twelfth Night* is considered the third of Shakespeare's most festive comedies. Here, too, the exclusion of one or more characters from the celebration at the close makes the conclusion more comprehensive, more universal in portraying the range of human responses and experiences. And in this instance, the primary holdout is Malvolio, the steward of Olivia's household. Unlike the neurotic Jaques, poor Malvolio does not reject the possibility of happiness. Indeed, he thinks it not an unreasonable prospect "to be Count Malvolio."

But in his case, he looks for happiness in the wrong places and is too self-absorbed and confident to realize his error. With these limitations in his nature, he will never grow in self-awareness, for his pride will come to the defense of his ego. The hurt and angry Malvolio storms offstage at the end of *Twelfth Night* shaking his fists and shouting, "I'll be revenged on the whole pack of you."

Yet Malvolio is not alone in his self-imposed exile. The doltish Sir Andrew Aguecheek and the sea captain, Antonio, are also excluded from the happy resolution. Sir Andrew never understood that he was simply a revenue source for Olivia's impoverished uncle, Sir Toby Belch. And although he saved Viola's twin brother from the shipwreck and offered him his "love without retention or restraint," the devoted Antonio has been displaced by Olivia. He, too, is rather an odd man out at the conclusion, with no place in the scheme of things. And so the joyous ending is tinged with melancholy, a mood conveyed by the song Feste sings.

The world established at the close of these mature comedies, with their range of characters and mixture of responses, is far more complex than what can be found at the end of such a play as *The Comedy of Errors*, a very early work in this genre. There, delight is universal and all-inclusive. But that is not typical of later Shakespearean comedy. Joy is rarely so enveloping as syrup on a pancake, covering all with sweetness. Shakespeare's urge to experiment with comedy, to extend the range of emotional responses it can dramatize, will gradually lead him away from creating works in which nearly all end happy into writing plays that are innovative hybrids. Although the so-called dark comedies, written shortly after *Twelfth Night*, may avoid death, tragic possibilities seem far too real to allow for much merriment.

Measure for Measure, one of these tragicomedies, has an especially daring, indeed extraordinary conclusion. In this case, the final resolution is not postponed, in the fashion of *Love's Labour's Lost*, or mixed, as in *Twelfth Night*, but left completely open. The audience is not presented with closure. We never learn what answer the heroine makes when she is asked by the Duke to "give me your hand and say you will be mine."

Some fifty lines later, in the last speech in the play, Duke Vincentio restates his proposal of marriage:

> Dear Isabel,
> I have a motion much imports your good,
> Whereto if you'll a willing ear incline,
> What's mine is yours, and what is yours is mine.
>
> (V.i)

Shakespeare has given us no preparation for this moment. Early in the action, the Duke claimed little interest in love and romance, thinking himself invulnerable to Cupid's arrow: "Believe not that the dribbling dart of love/ Can pierce a complete bosom." And Isabella, about to enter a cloister as a sister of the very strict Order of Saint Clare, is hardly a likely candidate for nuptials.

Yet the psychological preparation for the Duke's offer of marriage is not entirely lacking. Throughout the play, he has carefully watched Isabella's behavior at times of great stress and in the last scene has even tried her by his own rather deplorable deception. She is wrongly told that her brother has been executed by the deputy, Angelo. In this way, the Duke can test her response when he orders the same fate for the man responsible.

But Isabella does not seek revenge. Despite what seems a severe and cold nature, she ultimately proves more charitable and forgiving. She intercedes for Angelo's life arguing that since his attempted seduction of her was thwarted, he should not be punished for what he did not do:

> His act did not o'ertake his bad intent,
> And must be buried but as an intent
> That perished by the way. Thoughts are no subjects,
> Intents but merely thoughts.
>
> (V.i)

It is an important moment. Generosity of spirit is a commodity little seen in the world of this play until Isabella comes to embody it. And no doubt the Duke's appreciation of her remarkable nature is the motive that prompts him to ask for her hand.

Yet although she is addressed more than once, Isabella remains onstage, silent for the last ninety lines of the play. How does she react to the Duke's words, to his deception, and to his marriage proposal? Performance may prove the determining factor and different productions may provide different endings; a simple gesture by the actor playing Isabella will be enough to convey her response. Both possibilities—her acceptance or rejection—can be plausibly argued on psychological grounds, but a definitive answer is withheld. Shakespeare is silent. The intentional ambiguity or indeterminacy of his ending makes this play unique and intriguing.

The ending of *Hamlet* also raises insolvable questions about the nature of the hero's achievement and how we should respond to it.[37] On the one hand, he has accomplished what he set out to do. He established the truth of the ghost's accusation, he publicly proved his uncle's guilt, and he removed him from the throne. But on the other hand, Hamlet's course of action has led not only to his own death and that of his uncle but also to the deaths of Polonius, Gertrude, Laertes, and Ophelia as well as Rosencrantz and Guildenstern. And an even more questionable outcome is that the state of Denmark is left at the close with a new ruler, Fortinbras of Norway.

After all this, one might argue that had Hamlet been less heroic or dutiful he might perhaps have ignored the ghost's command and lived to become king of Denmark. His uncle publicly proclaimed Hamlet next in line for the throne:

> Think of us
> As of a father, for let the world take note,
> You are the most immediate to our throne.

(I.ii)

All Hamlet had to do was wait out the time, and Denmark would continue to be ruled by Danes.

Surely, the final resolution to the events of the play is bitterly ironic. Hamlet's father had fought and defeated the father of young Fortinbras, who bears his father's name. But with Prince Hamlet dying, the affairs of state are left so that "young Fortinbras, with conquests come from Poland," will not only "recover . . . those foresaid lands/ So by his father lost" but also take the crown of Denmark.

The play leaves us with a series of unresolved questions. Is this not a Pyrrhic victory, for has the price Hamlet paid to revenge his father's murder destroyed his country? How are we to consider his struggle and all the deaths that were a consequence of it? How do we reconcile the end of the play with the fact that Hamlet quotes from the Gospel of Matthew, "There's special providence in the fall of a sparrow"? Is Hamlet mistaken, or is the wisdom of heaven so remote and mysterious that it is incomprehensible to humankind? Is the play suggesting that victory and defeat are, perhaps, not so easy to distinguish, that winning and losing are not always opposite sides of the same coin?

The more one ponders the conclusion of *Hamlet*, the more one is left with a troubled reaction to the events and their outcome. The only way of dealing with these feelings is, of course, to go back and see the play again—no doubt just what the playwright and his company desired.

With *Richard II*, Shakespeare presents a different effect at the conclusion. Here the consequence of the action proves to be circular. Even after a civil war and a change in the monarchy, nothing is altered. The play closes with the country and crown in exactly the same situation, facing the same problems they confronted at the opening. At the start, Richard II, the hereditary king, must deal with discontented family members who bridle under his irresponsible rule and question his right to continue on the throne since he is implicated in the murder of his uncle, the Duke of Gloucester.

Richard's ambitious cousin, Henry Bolingbroke, presses the accusation. Since he cannot attack Richard directly, Bolingbroke un-

dermines the king by blaming Gloucester's death on Richard's
henchman, Thomas Mowbray. Richard clumsily tries to resolve his
difficulties by banishing both Bolingbroke and Mowbray, and then
compounds his mistakes by seizing his cousin's inheritance. Now
Bolingbroke has even stronger grounds for trying to unseat the
king, and the rebellion he leads gains support from all those who
fear that the king's arbitrary behavior could disenfranchise their
heirs. Ultimately, Richard is forced to abdicate, and Bolingbroke
becomes Henry IV.

But the new king has no hereditary right to the throne. As a consequence, those who soon feel that they have been ill-rewarded or
ill-used have an issue that will unite them against the new monarch.
Conspiracies to remove Henry IV are discovered, one involving
even his own cousin—exactly what occurred earlier. And in an effort to make Henry more secure, Sir Pierce of Exton, acting on be-
half of the new king, murders the imprisoned Richard.

So at the conclusion, Bolingbroke is very much like the cousin
he displaced: a ruler involved in the murder of a member of the
royal family who faces increasing hostility from the nobles. When
Exton appears in the last scene with Richard's coffin, he is, as was
Mowbray earlier, hardly a welcome sight to the man on the throne:

> BOLINGBROKE: Exton, I thank thee not; for thou hast
>   wrought
>   A deed of slander, with thy fatal hand,
>   Upon my head and all this famous land.
> EXTON: From your own mouth, my lord, did I this
>   deed.
> BOLINGBROKE: They love not poison that do poison need,
>   Nor do I thee. Though I did wish him dead,
>   I hate the murderer, love him murdered.
>
>   (V.vi)

As Mowbray was banished by Richard, so Exton is by Bolingbroke. At the play's conclusion, the situation is as it was at the
play's opening. Historical changes may be sweeping, but they leave
matters much as they were before.[38] How Bolingbroke will manage

as King Henry IV is left to a later work in the cycle of chronicle history plays, but in *Richard II*, with Exton's banishment, the wheel has surely come full circle.

The resolution to the more serious Shakespearean plays is problematic and intriguing, for rather than tying up all matters, the ending may instead raise new questions or demonstrate how persistent are the old ones. Life offers no absolute assurances and no permanent solutions; the way out of one problem inevitably raises others, usually not so very different from those met with earlier.

Tragedy requires the death of the hero, but comedy and history are less rigid genres. And so only a few Shakespearean plays—such as *The Comedy of Errors* and *A Midsummer Night's Dream*—end with happiness for all. And it is an equally unusual Shakespearean history that closes on an untroubled note. Even the "comical history" of *Henry IV, Part II,* ends with the arrest of Falstaff and the prospect of a war with France as a distraction from troubles at home.

In *Henry V,* the audience is reminded that the great successes of that "mirror of all Christian kings" were hardly long-lasting. All seems blissful by the last scene of the play: the young king has conquered France and with its princess as his "sovereign queen," the two countries "may cease their hatred" and "never war advance/ His bleeding sword 'twixt England and fair France." But this hope for a peaceful future is immediately denied by the final appearance of the Chorus. In his closing words he reminds the audience that with the death of Henry and the civil war that followed, the infant king, Henry the Sixth, "lost France and made his England bleed." Once again, peace is fragile, happiness ephemeral, and, as Hamlet says, "a man's life's no more than to say 'one.'" Individual character and personality may help shape the course of events, but, as Feste reminds the playgoer, ultimately "the whirligig of time brings in his revenges."

9

Conclusion: Why Shakespeare

In the poem he wrote to commemorate the first collected edition of Shakespeare's plays, Ben Jonson called his friend and rival the "soul of the age." But Jonson also understood that Shakespeare was not a playwright who spoke only to the English of the late sixteenth and early seventeenth centuries, for the poem goes on to call him a writer "not of an age, but for all time!" Jonson realized that Shakespeare was a phenomenon, a rarity, with the kind of creative talent that transcends his own society and his own historical period.

In Jonson's opinion, Shakespeare's talent was chiefly the ability to capture "nature's family" through vivid language and dramatize his material in carefully crafted works of art: "For though the poet's matter Nature be,/ His Art doth give the fashion." Jonson was thinking not only of the extraordinary range of characters in Shakespeare's comedies and tragedies but also of the playwright's constant experimentation in shaping his plots and putting them on the stage. In both the variety of people he created and the types of plays he wrote Shakespeare seems a phenomenon. No one, nature excepted, has succeeded in producing such different women as Juliet, Lady Macbeth, and Cleopatra, or such men as Romeo, Benedict, and King Lear. And rare is the playwright who is equally skilled at writing plays in so many genres.

Dramatic characters, of course, actually exist only as words on paper enacted on the stage, but for the writer the creative process must depend on language. And here Shakespeare had a formidable advantage. His vocabulary was immense: in his plays he used more than twenty-five thousand words. To give some idea of how extraordinary this is, we should bear in mind that John Milton, surely one of the most highly educated and well-read writers in the English language, uses a vocabulary of some twelve thousand words. In fact, more English words appear for the first time in the works of Shakespeare than any other writer. He is the first recorded user of hundreds of neologisms, some of which seem to be original with him ("dwindle," "courtship," "aerial," "leapfrog"). It is hardly an exaggeration to say that the language we speak today is in great measure his creation.

The extensiveness of his vocabulary is a great asset for a creative writer, but Shakespeare's greatness is not simply in the number of words he knew, but in writing about so many different characters, subjects, emotions, and situations that he needed to use so many words. Some of them are highly technical—terms of law, sailing, medicine, warfare, and heraldry; others are hardly surprising for a country lad—the language of hunting, gardening, flowers, and rural activities.

All of this can be attributed to an enormously quick, curious, and retentive mind. His memory must have been prodigious. Shakespeare lived when new words were becoming current at a greater rate than at any other time in the history of England, a consequence of global commerce and travel, of a new openness to the world at large, and of the study of classical literature—Latin comedies and Virgil were a part of the Stratford school curriculum. Shakespeare listened to the conversations being spoken all around him; he remembered what he heard and how these words were used; and he incorporated this new vocabulary in the dialogue of his characters.

This facility with language was managed with great skill, for Shakespeare's dialogue can be understood sufficiently both to follow the action and grasp the elements of the characters without knowing precisely each word that is spoken. Modern audiences are occasionally surprised to discover that they readily understand Shakespearean dialogue when they hear it spoken, yet have some difficulty when they try reading it. The actor's intonation, tone of voice, and gesture as well as the context in which a speech is delivered all help make the meaning clear; synonyms are often included and thoughts restated so that the attentive listener will have no problem with comprehension. After all, for Shakespeare's audience some of this vocabulary was also new, and reading was not a widespread skill.

So Shakespeare chose his words with great care, deliberately mixing the Latinate with the Anglo-Saxon, the multisyllabic with the direct, one-syllable word to convey ideas and feelings. When Lady Macbeth encourages her husband to think that a little water will clear them of their deed, he stands aghast, staring at his blood-smeared body and crying out: "No, this my hand will rather/ The multitudinous seas incarnadine,/ Making the green one red." The meaning of the Latinate word "incarnadine" is implied in the line that follows. The multisyllabic weightiness of "multitudinous" and "incarnadine" convey the heavy burden of guilt that staggers Macbeth, while the words "green" and "red," Anglo-Saxon in origin, restate the meaning and in their brevity bring a sense of finality.

Simply knowing lots of words does not, of course, make one an artist at putting them in memorable combinations. But that, too, was a talent Shakespeare had to an unparalleled degree. Although what he says may not be especially original, his phrasing is so congenial, so memorable, that it has become common currency. Such phrases as "barefaced lie," "a foregone conclusion," "in the pink," and "the mind's eye" seem so natural that we fail to realize someone actually had to think them up. Word combinations and language choices also reflect considerations of rank and position, age and class. Shakespeare enjoys mixing kings and clowns, high and low art, blank verse and prose.

By their choice of language Shakespeare's characters reveal themselves. Their dialogue reflects how they respond to the world. Shakespeare would have to keep in mind how one character would address another and what vocabulary would be appropriate. Such thoughts about what sort of language to use are actually expressed by Sir Walter Blunt in *Henry IV, Part One,* when he attempts to defend Hotspur's rudeness on the battlefield. Sir Walter argues that one must excuse Hotspur's angry words by taking into account what was said "to such a person, and in such a place,/ At such a time."

The ability to see the world through the eyes of his characters and to find a language that reflects their personalities is an essential part of Shakespeare's genius as a dramatist. The Earl of Gloucester blames the problems arising in Lear's kingdom on the "late eclipses in the sun and moon." This is a conservative, traditional view of the correspondences that relate everything to everything else, that the macrocosm and microcosm are interconnected. Such thinking could be expected from someone of Gloucester's generation. His illegitimate son, Edmund, however, is aware of the new ideas that were to find expression in the writing of men such as Galileo and Machiavelli. So Edmund believes he is independent of "heavenly compulsion" and privately argues that, as a totally free agent, he is unconstrained by any moral or familial obligations: "I should have been that I am had the maidenliest star in the firmament twinkled on my bastardizing." Alone on stage he congratulates himself on his cleverness and resolves that nothing should stand in his way.

Shakespeare's skill at finding a language and point of view appropriate for each character is enhanced by his ability to sustain different attitudes toward life, to give them equal voice, and to allow them to express their truths with equal weight. In *The Tempest*, when Miranda first sees the King of Naples and his attendants, she is struck by the sight of so many distinguished visitors to the island where she has grown up away from the rest of society.

> O wonder!
> How many goodly creatures are there here!
> How beauteous mankind is. O brave new world
> That has such people in't!
>
> (V.i)

But she is unaware that these visitors are her uncle and the King of Naples, men who unseated her father as Duke of Milan and endangered both their lives. Prospero has not forgotten this, for he has just admitted that he cannot bring himself to call Antonio his "brother." So Prospero's answer to his daughter's exclamation of surprise and delight is a more weary and cynical rejoinder: "'Tis new to thee." Her innocent optimism is countered by his worldly skepticism.

Both responses are in keeping with those who speak them, and neither one cancels out the other. Shakespeare knows that at times we find this a "brave new world," and he realizes that at other moments and at other ages we may, speaking with the voice of experience, simply tell the young, "'Tis new to thee."

Such a skeptical attitude is characteristic of this playwright who is fascinated by multiple possibilities, doubtful that any absolute truth can ever be established, and deeply curious about people and what motivates them. He well knows that subjectivity affects all human responses. In *Troilus and Cressida*, the young Troilus argues "what's aught but as 'tis valued"—the worth of any object is simply how much one is willing to pay for it—and he comes to acknowledge that subjective reactions inevitably color our judgment, for what he thinks of Cressida cannot ultimately be reconciled with what he sees her do.

At its bleakest, Shakespeare's view of life is dark indeed and open to despair. In *Richard II*, when the Duke of York is asked for solace and encouragement, he responds, "I should belie my thoughts./ Comfort's in heaven, and we are on the earth." Or in *King Lear*, Albany's call to heaven for Cordelia's safety, "The gods defend her," is answered by the stage direction: "Enter Lear, with Cordelia in his arms" as the old king appears struggling to bear the lifeless body of his youngest daughter. The tortured and blinded Gloucester may well think himself the victim of sadistic powers: "As flies to wanton boys are we to th' gods;/ They kill us for their sport." But he later agrees with a less harshly negative view of life, the philosophy of stoic acceptance, of fortitude and endurance propounded by Edgar: "Men must endure/ Their going hence, even as their coming hither;/ Ripeness is all."

But the words of these characters reflect only their own thoughts. Shakespeare's works propose not simply that we accept what life offers but celebrate it as well. Lear's capacity for growth and development as well as Cordelia's absolute dedication are reasons for wonder and praise. The ways of heaven are mysterious.

After terrible misfortunes and depression, when Pericles is miraculously reunited with his wife and daughter, he tells the gods, "Your present kindness/ Makes my past miseries sports." Jupiter says in *Cymbeline*:

> Be not with mortal accidents opprest.
> No care of yours it is; you know 'tis ours
> Whom best I love I cross: to make my gift,
> The more delayed, delighted. Be content.
>
> (V.iv)

Without the suffering and delay, the happiness that follows can never be felt so intensely. In *The Winter's Tale*, after sixteen years of separation, giving him time enough to repent, Leontes is reunited with the queen he thought he had lost. Paulina addresses the "statue" and Hermione stirs.

Shakespeare is a playwright who never speaks in his own voice. Instead, he gives his actors the language of the characters they play. William Hazlitt, the early nineteenth-century essayist and literary critic, put this thought well: Shakespeare "was the least of an egotist that it was possible to be. He was nothing in himself, but he was all that others were, or that they could become."[39] Even his sonnets, which are often thought his most personal writing, are too restricted by convention and form to be considered deeply revelatory.

Yet we can learn something of the playwright's own interests and attitudes by looking at other writers whose attitudes he found congenial. Two of Shakespeare's favorites books were Plutarch's *Lives of the Noble Grecians and Romans Compared Together* (in a translation by Thomas North) and Michel de Montaigne's *Essays* (in a translation by John Florio). He knew the work of both men well and drew upon them for source material as well as inspiration. In fact, the two have much in common. Both were fascinated by human nature and the wellsprings of action.

Shakespeare's history plays are deeply indebted to Plutarch's *Lives*, for the biographer explained that he wished to write:

[not] histories but only lives. For the noblest deeds do not always show men's virtues and vices, but oftentimes a light occasion, a word, or some sport makes men's natural dispositions and manners appear more plain than the famous battles won, wherein are slain 10,000 men, or the great armies or cities won by siege or assault.

Rather than write about the lives of famous Greeks and Romans like Plutarch, Montaigne arrived at a radically different subject: "I am myself the matter of my book." Thinking of himself as representative of humanity and subjecting his self-analysis to critical judgment, he tries in his *Essays* to arrive at an understanding not only of his own nature but of mankind as well. Essential truths of humanity and of the ethical issues that confront us become more sharply defined in the course of his introspection. Moreover, Montaigne argues, since our knowledge is inevitably partial, biased, and short-lived, a prey to private passions and weaknesses, how can we be anything but skeptical and stoic; how can we fail to take account of other points of view and other possibilities since our own senses give us so limited an understanding of a truth that is seldom a single surety?

This attitude allowed Montaigne to look at life with bemused optimism, with an awareness, for example, that limitations are not always obstacles to happiness. On the contrary, he would argue, obstacles may make a hard-won happiness all the sweeter. This response reminds one of Jupiter's words in *Cymbeline* explaining that delayed happiness can yield even more intense delight.

So Shakespeare's skepticism also seems fundamentally optimistic. And like Montaigne, he is responsive to the beauty of nature, sensitive to the rich diversity of experience, and aware of the need for generosity and understanding. Montaigne's words in his essay "Of Experience" would have struck a sympathetic chord with Shakespeare:

Our life is composed like the harmony of the world, of contrary things, also of different tones, sweet and harsh, sharp and flat, soft and loud. If a musician liked only one kind, what would he have to say? He must know how to use them together and blend them. And

so must we do with good and evil, which are consubstantial with
our life. Our being is impossible without this mixture, and one element is no less necessary for it than the other.

And, like Montaigne, Shakespeare was obsessed with the passage
of time, with the realization of the effects of constant change. Montaigne wrote: "I do not portray being: I portray passing . . . from
day to day, from minute to minute." For Shakespeare, we can never
escape from past time. Henry IV is always burdened by the memory of the "bypaths and indirect crooked ways" through which he
became king, and his guilt is bequeathed to his son. On the morn-
ing of the battle at Agincourt, Henry V prays: "Not to-day, O
Lord,/ O not today, think not upon the fault/ My father made in
compassing the crown!"

An awareness of the brevity of life, indebted to the past yet made
up of fleeting moments that vanish in an instant and can never be
recaptured, is a constant element in the plays. Youth and passion,
pleasure and high spirits, deep affection and abiding love can all
become matters of a moment. Even in *As You Like It,* in the Forest
of Arden, the land of the pastoral where nature is supposed to be
sweet and humanity young, where men "fleet the time carelessly as
they did in the golden world," Rosalind warns Orlando that in
matters of romance, "Say a day, without the ever." Touchstone remarks how "from hour to hour, we ripe and ripe,/ And then, from
hour to hour, we rot and rot." And Jaques finds life to end in "mere
oblivion . . . sans everything." In *Twelfth Night*, Feste reminds us
that "youth's a stuff will not endure." And the disguised Viola,
who cannot directly admit her love for Orsino, tells him that she
knows the cost of unrequited affection by describing her feelings
and attributing them to a fictitious sister:

> She never told her love,
> But let concealment like a worm i'th'bud,
> Feed on her damask cheek. She pined in thought;
> And with a green and yellow melancholy,
> She sat like Patience on a monument,
> Smiling at grief. Was not this love indeed?

(II.iv)

The hilarity and high spirits of *Love's Labour's Lost* are suddenly dissipated, like an unexpected shadow blocking the brightest sunlight, when a stranger dressed in black, Monsieur Marcade, appears unannounced late in the last act to bring news of the French king's death. As Berowne realizes, "The scene begins to cloud." In the few remaining moments of the play before the Princess must leave for her own country, "the latest minute of the hour," there is not time enough for a true exchange of vows, "a world-without-end bargain." All at once the moment has passed, the mood is somber, and the joy has vanished. The play closes with the songs of winter and spring with their refrain of "when" and "then" reminding us of the continuity of life even as our own lives are changing. Indeed, the change is so abrupt, so unprepared, that it is rather like Prospero's shout to his spirits, "Avoid! No more!" Then, unexpectedly, with a clap of his hands, the wedding masque in *The Tempest* is over, and we learn that "our revels now are ended."

As these examples suggest, Shakespeare writes a great deal not only about time but also about love. He is clearly interested in the many forms that it takes and the guises in which it is manifested, whether youthful and exuberant (*Romeo and Juliet*); proud and sensitive (*Much Ado About Nothing*); repressed and somewhat psychotic (*Measure for Measure*); anguished and remorseful (*Macbeth*); mother-fixated and self-destructive (*Coriolanus*); passionate and all-consuming (*Antony and Cleopatra*); parental and filial (*King Lear*.)

Perhaps love is so important a subject in his work because happiness in Shakespeare's world seems rather impossible without it. And from recognizing the essential importance of love, he moves on to acknowledge that happiness also often demands forgiveness, both of one's own foolishness and that of others. The romantic comedies of the first half of his career evolve into the romances written toward the end of it, plays in which young love becomes entwined with matters of family reconciliation. Even as he angrily remembers the evil and cruelty of his brother, Prospero realizes that though vengeance is sweet, a different course of action is to be preferred:

> Though with their high wrongs I am struck to th'quick
> Yet with my nobler reason 'gainst my fury
> Do I take part: the rarer action is
> In virtue than in vengeance: they being penitent,
> The sole drift of my purpose doth extend
> Not a frown further.

> (V.i)

We can hear a restatement of these sentiments in Lear's plea to Cordelia: "I pray you, now, forget and forgive/ I am old and foolish." Lear now knows that even in a prison he would sing like a bird in a cage if he can be with her and share in her love: to "take upon's the mystery of things/ As if we were God's spies."

With his powerful language, fascinating characters, and engaging stories Shakespeare has fulfilled Jonson's prediction for over four centuries: his writing is "not for an age but for all time."

Indeed, the continued widespread interest in Shakespeare both in the theater and the classroom is not a reflection of the position of the English language as a medium of global communication, nor is the playwright's reputation a consequence of his adoption as the standard-bearer of British imperialism. Nor are his influence and importance simply a result of his place in the educational curriculum. Such arguments confuse cause and effect. Shakespeare's popularity is due to the power of his writing, to the effect that his works have on an audience, to their truth to human nature, and to the way their poetry communicates human feelings. It is his artistry and intelligence that explain this dominance, not social, or pedagogical, or geopolitical issues. Ben Jonson was right again when he sang his rival's praises. After all, he knew the man and saw his plays when they were first performed:

> Thou art a Monument without a tomb
> And art alive still, while thy Book doth live,
> And we have wits to read, and praise to give.

Afterword

On the Publication and Performance of the Plays

Especially in the last century, scholars have learned a great deal about Shakespeare's biography, education, and career as well as about the contemporary theater. In fact, we have today no rational or logical reason to doubt Shakespeare's authorship of the plays usually attributed to him. Indeed, the claim that he was not the real author occurred in print for the first time only in the mid-nineteenth century, the wildly argued proposal of an American woman who was mentally unbalanced. None of Shakespeare's contemporaries ever doubted his dramatic and poetic creativity—even those envious of his success.

Those who knew him best professionally could comment with authority on his facility and genius, for they witnessed it in action. Unlike the modern theater, acting companies in Shakespeare's day had no one who functioned as a director. Since Shakespeare appeared in the plays he wrote—he seems to have cast himself in small supporting roles—his fellow actors would naturally have turned to him during rehearsals of a new work for advice and explanations on how a particular scene should be performed, on the way a line should be delivered, or on the meaning of some unfamiliar word or phrase. If the action was confusing or the meaning of the dialogue was unclear, the players had only to ask the playwright for clarification.

If Shakespeare were not the real author but only the front for another writer, this would have quickly become apparent; he would not have been able to answer every question of meaning or staging that the company might ask. And so very many people would have been aware of the fact that it could hardly be kept a secret for long. Yet there was never any doubt then or even for centuries after about who created the works that bear his name.

Shakespeare first appears in theatrical history in the early 1590s, when he was in his late twenties; by 1594, when the theaters re-opened after a severe epidemic of the plague, he and Richard Bur-bage were principal members of an acting company known as "the Lord Chamberlain's Men." All acting troupes in England needed a patron or sponsor; as nominal members of the household staff of an aristocratic family or royalty, a company of players would be licensed to travel and hoped to profit from the influence of their protector.

The Lord Chamberlain's Men became one of the principal com-panies. They were an unusually stable group of actors. Although the membership of the Lord Chamberlain's Players changed very little, the troupe was given a new name, becoming the "King's Men," when James VI of Scotland succeeded Elizabeth as monarch in 1603 and became their patron.

In 1599, when they left the public playhouse known as the The-atre for a new one, the Globe, erected on the south bank of the Thames, five of the Lord Chamberlain's players formed a joint partnership. By investing in the real-estate and construction costs of the new building, they became business shareholders, so their mutual interests were both financial and artistic, further strength-ening their bonds. And when, about 1609, the company began to make use of the indoor theater called the Blackfriars, the same ar-rangement was adopted. William Shakespeare was an investor in both playhouses.

Shakespeare created on average two plays a year for the Lord Chamberlain's Men. He wrote only for them. The advantages for both writer and actors were multiple. They had as their exclusive author the man who was acknowledged as the most important playwright in the contemporary theatre, and he had not only a high degree of stability as actor/writer but also the advantage of knowing well the talents and specialties of the men for whom he wrote. In *Much Ado About Nothing*, Shakespeare had in mind the particular actors in his company who would be playing the various parts, for in one scene rather than indicating the names of the play's characters, the Constable Dogberry and his partner Verges, Shakespeare actually uses the names of the actors, "Kemp" and "Cowley," as speech-prefixes. William Kemp was the company's principal clown at this time; he was probably the original Falstaff as well as Dogberry, two similar characters, larger-than-life, voluble, imperious, robust, and irrepressible. This was Kemp's well-defined role. Yet for so versatile an actor as Richard Burbage, Shakespeare created such diverse and challenging heroes as Hamlet, Othello, and Lear, men different in age and temperament.

A London company such as the Lord Chamberlain's consisted of some eight to twelve men, "sharers" who divided up costs and profits. With the agreement of the shareholders, an actor could buy or sell shares in a company. In addition to the sharers, three or four boys were needed to play the women's parts and some half dozen extras to perform the smaller roles as well as musicians and backstage help. All in all, most plays required a cast of about twenty, even though roles were doubled where possible.

A repertory system was common among the London troupes. A different play was presented at each performance, and new works were introduced frequently. At the public playhouses in the mid-1590s, for example, when they were performing six days a week, the adult companies presented just under forty different plays in a season. Slightly more than half their repertory were new works, so the companies had a constant and urgent need for fresh material. In addition, the pressure on the actors must have been considerable. Their ability to memorize quickly seems to border on the phenomenal: a leading actor had constantly to add new roles and recall old ones. By one estimate, in a three-year period, a principal member of the Lord Admiral's company "had to secure and retain command of about seventy-one different roles, of which number fifty-two or fifty-three were newly learned."[40]

Acting companies presented their works in three different settings. The large, open-air playhouses in London such as the Globe or the Rose were round or multi-sided timber structures about seventy-two feet in diameter. Some two thousand five hundred spectators could stand in the yard around the stage for a penny, or for an additional penny enter one of the three galleries that ringed the sides of the building, or for yet more money sit in greater comfort in the higher galleries. The stage extended from one side of the building nearly into the middle of the yard. A changing room was located behind it; two or more doors opened from this "tiring house" onto the stage. The first gallery level on this wall of the building could be used during a performance as Juliet's balcony, or as Cleopatra's tomb, or as the ramparts on the top of a walled town. From the top of this façade and supported on two columns that stood on the stage, a cover, known as the "heavens" because of the way it was painted, extended over the playing-area to protect the actors (and their expensive costumes) from inclement weather. In addition, a pulley located in the small "hut" above the cover provided the means for raising and lowering actors through the cover onto the stage. In this way, a god or spirit could ascend to paradise or descend to earth. The hut also housed the musicians and the sound-effects machinery. Music was usually called for during these transitions from earth to heaven in order to mask the noise of the pulley system. A large trapdoor was cut into the stage near the center front where such moments as the graveyard scene in *Hamlet* could be staged.

At the western edge of the city walls in the Blackfriars precinct of London, an indoor commercial playhouse was created in the 1570s where a company of children from one of the choir schools performed. This ultimately became a second performance home for the adult acting companies. After the children's companies went out of business, Burbage and five members of the King's Men, Shakespeare included, remodeled the building to create an enclosed playing space 66′ × 46′ in the paved hall of the old Blackfriars priory. This was a candlelighted, more exclusive entertainment venue. The capacity of such a private playhouse was less than half that of the outdoor public theaters—"perhaps no more than five or six hundred" spectators—though the box-office receipts were much greater since the ticket prices "were at least six times as high." The audience here was no doubt more fashionable and wealthy than that found in the larger open-air playhouses, attended by a greater cross section of the residents of and visitors to London. More men than women were in the audience, but women were present, the respectable ones accompanied by male escorts.[41]

Some of the performance elements were similar to those of the public playhouse—a stage was set up at one end, a heaven for raising and lowering actors was installed, a mid-stage trap existed, and the space provided a raised window or balcony playing-area. The principal difference between the two playing venues was "not so much the design of the stage area as the layout of the auditorium."[42]

Finally, acting companies, reduced in size to cut back on their costs, toured the countryside during the summer months when the theaters were often closed because the number of deaths from the plague increased in the warm weather. (The London authorities banned large gatherings in the mistaken belief that the plague was contagious.) Under these circumstances, the players had not only to reshuffle their text to accommodate their reduced numbers but also to adapt their staging to whatever was available. An inn yard, any makeshift space to which admission could be controlled, could readily be turned into a performance space.

Professional companies also acted before private audiences. *The Comedy of Errors* was first presented before the lawyers of Gray's Inn as a part of their Christmas Revels in 1594; *Twelfth Night* was performed before the gentlemen of the Middle Temple, another one of the Inns of Court, on February 2, 1602; and *The Merry Wives of Windsor* may have been seen first at Westminster during the feast of the Knights of the Garter in 1597. Invitations to give performances at court as part of the Christmas holidays or on special occasions were also welcome, for the rewards were generous and the publicity desirable. In the winter season of 1604–5, Shakespeare's company was invited to present many of his plays to the new royal family. These include *Othello, Measure for Measure, Henry V,* and *The Merchant of Venice*, which was acted a second time by royal command. The players traveled to wherever the court was located—Greenwich, Whitehall, Hampton Court. And when the aristocracy entertained, they, too, invited the actors.

A play such as *Love's Labour's Lost*, for example, has an extensive and varied history. It was acted at both the Globe and the Blackfriars, according to one title page, performed before Queen Elizabeth at Christmas in 1597, staged at the Earl of Southampton's London house in 1604 (to celebrate his release from prison), and revived for King James's consort, Queen Anne, in the same year. Adaptability in staging and performing was obviously the rule; flexibility in meeting the restrictions and limitations of various playing spaces and facilities was perhaps an acting company's key requirement.

To suit the occasion—which could involve a reduced number of players, or limited facilities, or changes in the cast—the texts could be adjusted as needed. Shakespeare could hardly object since the common practice was that the acting company bought the script from the author. In any case, he seems to have had no interest in overseeing the printing of his works for the stage. To maintain control the companies preferred not to allow their plays to appear in print form. When a play no longer attracted a large enough audience to warrant revival or when a company needed to raise cash, they might then sell their script to a publisher.

The manuscript turned over to a printer could have had several sources. It might be the author's original draft ("foul papers," as they were known,) or his "fair copy." Inconsistencies in the naming of characters and vague and inaccurate stage directions are characteristic, especially of foul papers. Both of these texts became the possession of the acting company when they made their final payment for the play. Or the manuscript turned over to the printing house could be one prepared for performance by the acting company's scribe, with complete and accurate stage directions. Some of the texts of Shakespeare's plays were printed from versions prepared by Ralph Crane, the scribe for the King's Men, whose work can be identified by his idiosyncratic spelling and contractions.

Eighteen of Shakespeare's plays appeared first printed in quarto form. A quarto, roughly 9″ × 14″, has four pages printed on each side of a sheet. The sheet is then folded twice, making four leaves (i.e., a quarto) so that the four leaves become eight pages. Of course, the manuscript source for printing a quarto could be any one of the three mentioned above, or the quarto might even be based on a text cobbled together illegitimately. The first quarto (or Q1) of *Hamlet* was surely published from a version of the play that is only distantly related to what Shakespeare wrote and his company actually performed. It may well have been the product of an actor or actors who were not shareholders in the company; hired to play minor roles, such men tried to reconstruct the work from memory, invent what they could not recall, and sell their creation as the one "diverse times acted by His Highness Servants in the City of London." Shakespeare's company evidently responded to this fraud by speedily authorizing another printing of the play, which, according to the title page, is "enlarged to almost as much again as it was, according to the true and perfect copy." This is known as Q2. By one illicit means or another, several of Shakespeare's plays, such as *Romeo and Juliet* and *Henry V,* appeared in unauthorized versions.

In 1623, six years after Shakespeare died, two of his former colleagues in the King's Men, John Heminges and Henry Condell, published his collected works in a folio edition. (Heminges and Condell, along with Richard Burbage, are the only three members of the acting company named in Shakespeare's will.) Although the handmade paper sheets used by printers varied in size, a folio is easily distinguished from a quarto since it is a very much larger book: two pages are printed on each side of a single sheet, which is then folded only once to become four pages.

Of the thirty-six plays in this *First Folio,* eighteen had never appeared in print. Heminges and Condell in their preface claim that even those texts that were "maimed and deformed" now appear "cured and perfect of their limbs, and all the rest absolute in their numbers, as he conceived them." The *Folio* does include *Henry VIII,* which Shakespeare wrote with John Fletcher, but it does not contain two others they wrote jointly, *The Two Noble Kinsmen,* published later in quarto, or *Cardenio,* now lost. *Pericles,* another play that involves collaboration, is also missing from the *Folio.*

The printer's copy for the eighteen previously unpublished plays could be any of those three manuscript sources discussed above, or a combination of them. Of the eighteen plays that had appeared in print, the quarto was often supplemented by referring to a manuscript version of the same play. None of Shakespeare's original papers for material in the *First Folio* is extent.

In some cases, the quarto and the Folio versions of a play offer different readings, and both can seem authentically Shakespearean. The quarto of *King Lear* published in 1608, for example, which is a relatively sound text, offers some three hundred lines that are not in the Folio, and the Folio version contains nearly a hundred lines not in the quarto. Possibly Shakespeare reworked the play; perhaps he was motivated by artistic reasons or he may have made alterations for practical ones.

The two versions of *Hamlet* present a similar problem: Q2 has 230 lines not in the Folio, and the Folio has seventy lines not in Q2. Perhaps the play needed cutting. But Hamlet's famous soliloquy, "How all occasions do inform against me," which appears in Q2, is omitted in the Folio text. A reader of any edition of these plays will either have to rely on the judgment of the editor, or, as is more and more common now for some plays, modern editors provide both versions of the same play, often on facing pages.

Establishing a single, ideal, perfect, and complete text of a Shakespearean play, reprinting each and every word just as the author wrote it, is clearly an impossibility, for the author sometimes provided alternate versions. Errors could also creep in at every stage of the printing process. Misreading the manuscript—and Shakespeare's handwriting might not have been easily deciphered—setting the type incorrectly, misjudging the allocation of space so that the lines on a page are cut or compressed are all established causes of error.

Even when textual difficulties are not the result of manuscripts or printing-house problems, other factors may be responsible. An example involving *Measure for Measure* will illustrate this point. According to documents in the Public Records Office, this play was performed at court during the Christmas season of 1604–5. No quarto version was printed; the only text is that in the *First Folio* of

1623. These dates are important to keep in mind, for they may well have affected the language. When in soliloquy Angelo admits that even as he prays he cannot help thinking of the young woman he has just met, his word choice seems odd:

> When I would pray and think, I think and pray
> To several subjects: Heaven hath my empty words,
> Whilst my invention, hearing not my tongue,
> Anchors on Isabel: Heaven in my mouth,
> As if I did but only chew his name . . .
>
> (III.iv)

The word in his mouth would more appropriately be "God" rather than "Heaven," for then "chew his name" would have a referent.

This substitution of "Heaven" for "God" is probably a consequence of the *Act to Restrain Abuses of Players,* which Parliament passed in 1606. According to this legislation, enacted to discourage actors from speaking profanely (and voicing political criticism), members of an audience who reported them for swearing or voicing references to God on stage would receive the fines the actors would have to pay. As a consequence, the players excised the prohibited vocabulary from the dialogue, and acceptable substitutes, such as "heaven," were put in their place. Shakespeare's line with an inexact referent has been recast to keep the acting company safe from penalty, or, as he expresses it in *Twelfth Night,* "o' th' windy side of the law." So even in the case of a play that exists only in one printed version and that version set into type from a clean manuscript probably prepared by the company's professional scribe, the wording is not assuredly in every instance exactly what the playwright first wrote.

The textual history of Shakespeare's plays is a fascinating subject for scholars, but the enjoyment of them is a pleasure available to all. Moreover, since Shakespeare presents the action through several different points of view and manages to favor none, his works are almost endlessly open to interpretation. Fresh readings, radical productions, and constant reinvention are always possible with Shakespeare's dramas. He knows that truth is never determinable as single, absolute, and unchanging, but rather that it is variable, subject to person, time, and place. For this reason the plays can be made relevant to any audience anywhere.[43]

Until the early twentieth century, the texts of Shakespeare's plays were treated with a good deal of freedom. Alterations were so common that the works became largely the fantasies of various actors and theater managers who adapted them as they saw fit.

A Midsummer Night's Dream is a perfect example of this phenomenon. When Samuel Pepys saw the play in September, 1662, it was so cut and revised that he thought it "the most insipid, ridiculous play that ever I saw in my life." The evening was redeemed for him only "by some good dancing, and some handsome women, which was all my pleasure." Musical enrichment had become an essential part of the play's presentation. In fact, before the end of the seventeenth century, Thomas Betterton, with the help of the composer Henry Purcell, turned *A Midsummer Night's Dream* into an opera, *The Fairy Queen* (1692). David Garrick followed in this mode by presenting the play as an extravaganza entitled *The Fairies* (1755) with twenty-eight songs. Only the lovers, the fairies, and some six hundred of Shakespeare's lines survived his version of the text.

A Midsummer Night's Dream had become an occasion for a theatrical spectacle. In her 1840 production, Mme. Vestris, who took the part of Oberon and sang nine songs, restored most of Shakespeare's lines, but the action was still overwhelmed by the masses of fairies, by the elaborate, antiquarian stage designs, and by the busy stage effects she thought necessary. The popularity of Mendelssohn's incidental music, composed in 1843, also contributed to the custom of presenting the play as part opera and part ballet, a tradition that lasted well into the twentieth century in the stage presentations of Beerbohm Tree (1900; 1911) and Max Reinhardt (1905–1939). Bernard Shaw's judgment of an 1895 production can stand for all these elaborate stage spectacles. Shaw realized the consequence of all the music, sets, and extras to the staging: "Every accessory . . . is brought in at the deadliest risk of destroying the magic spell woven by the poet." Ultimately, the extravaganza en-

acted before the audience "is more absurd than anything that occurs in the tragedy of Pyramus and Thisbe in the last act."[44]

The first modern effort to perform the full text *of A Midsummer
Night's Dream* in a direct and uncut production was undertaken
by Harley Granville-Barker in 1914. Male actors once again played
Oberon and Puck, and Mendelssohn's music was replaced by English folk melodies. But it was not until Peter Brook's 1970 production that the play was entirely rethought. Brook's version
catapulted Shakespeare's play onto the stage in an immediate and
direct manner, conveying its sense of joy and wonder. This interpretation broke so radically with the past that it astonished audiences, who responded enthusiastically to the strangeness and
surprises that they saw onstage. The director set the action in a
three-sided white box; Bottom was something of circus clown; the
fairy queen's bower was an enormous red feather; the fairies swung
on trapezes; and the roles of Theseus and Hippolyta were doubled
with those of Oberon and Titania. The wedding march from Mendelssohn's music was parodied, and, all in all, the sexual undercur-
rents of the play were strongly emphasized. This radical treatment
conveyed something of both the joyousness of the work and its disturbing psychic energy, its libidinousness. Brook was speaking to
a new age. After two world wars, the collapsing of empires, and the
psychic probing of Freud, the later half of the twentieth century
was in need of a fresh start and a new beginning. This treatment of
Shakespeare's play gave voice to the mood of the moment.[45]

Two totally different film versions of *Henry V* will also demonstrate this point. Undertaken during some of the worst years of
World War II, Sir Laurence Olivier directed and starred in a film
version dedicated to the Royal Air Force and intended to bolster
national morale. Olivier's is a stirring, patriotic reading of the play:
the actor, resplendent and heroic on his white horse, leads the British forces successfully "once more unto the breach." At the time
of its release in November, 1944, this became the most successful
motion picture in British screen history.[46] And in 1947, Olivier
won an Academy Award "for his outstanding achievement" in this
film. In 1989, forty-five years later, in the post–Vietnam period
when war had proved a very disillusioning memory, a young Brit-

ish actor, Kenneth Branagh, directed and starred in his own motion picture version. His *Henry V* emphasizes the pain and suffering caused by armed conflict and the high cost of victory. Branagh is a tired and dirty Henry V at Agincourt as he leads his sick and weary troops through muddy fields and chilling rain. And once again, Branagh, as the film's director and lead actor, was awarded an Academy Award. Both films respect the text, yet they yield totally different interpretations.

Shakespeare's plays are capable of offering talented directors and performers an inexhaustible number of readings. And as we might expect, all actors worth their salt feel the challenge of making their mark on stage in such parts as Hamlet, Lear, and Prospero or as Rosalind, Lady Macbeth, and Cleopatra, for these are the roles by which the members of their profession are measured.

Some of this creativity on the part of directors and actors is the consequence of new critical approaches to the plays. Freud's essay on Hamlet and the oedipal complex, mentioned in chapter 6, is only one example of the way that a particular psychological approach can make the case for reading a character in a certain light. But applying Jacques Lacan's more recent writings on questions of identity and self-consciousness to the hero will naturally lead critics to other explanations for his behavior.

Over the last several years, literary scholars have applied a dizzying number of theoretical methodologies. Some turn to linguistics and study the ways that words serve as signs and symbols in order to enrich the meaning of Shakespeare's poetry; in this way they offer new and sometimes controversial interpretations. Structuralism and deconstruction are critical approaches that look closely at the ways a story is shaped and the elements of its plotting to arrive at a distinctive understanding of a work. Drawing on anthropological and cultural studies, "cultural poetics" or "the new historicism" are literary studies that often argue for new analyses of Shakespeare's texts as commenting on society, the political order, and its power structure in covertly critical or even subversive ways. Feminist as well as gay and lesbian scholars highlight still other aspects of Shakespearean characters and the ways they interact. And reader-response critics direct attention to the idiosyncrasies of each reader whose unique responses lead to multiple and irreconcilable interpretations of the same text. In sum, this near frenzy of differing methodologies, doctrines, and practices has produced "much throwing about of brains," to use Shakespeare's words in *Hamlet*.

But all of this proves once again the openness of these plays to new approaches and their freshness to a new generation. As Heminges and Condell tell us in their prefatory note to the *First Folio*, the playwright, "as he was a happy imitator of Nature, was a most gentle expresser of it," so that his genius, or "wit," "can no more lie hid than it could be lost." All we need bring to his plays are a curious mind and an attentive ear, and Shakespeare will admit us to a world like ours, but one far more engrossing, entertaining, and life-enhancing.

NOTES

1. Geoffrey Bullough, ed. *Narrative and Dramatic Sources of Shake-speare* (London, 1957–75).

2. T. W. Baldwin, *William Shakspere's Small Latine & Lesse Greek* (Urbana, 1944) as well as his *Shakespeare's Five-Act Structure* (Urbana, 1963).

3. *"To the Great Variety of Readers,"* prefatory remarks to the *First Folio* by John Heminges and Henry Condell.

4. See Steven Urkowitz, *Shakespeare's Revision of "King Lear"* (Princeton, 1980) and Gary Taylor and Michael Warren, *The Division of the Kingdoms: Shakespeare's Two Versions of 'King Lear'* (Oxford, 1983).

5. Samuel Johnson, *Preface to Shakespeare*, in *Shakespeare Criticism 1623–1840*, ed. D. Nichol Smith (London, 1961), p.93.

6. "Expectation in preference to surprise" is how Coleridge describes this distinguishing element of Shakespearean drama in his "Recapitulation and Summary of the Characteristics of Shakspeare's Dramas." D. Nichol Smith, ed. *Shakespearean Criticism 1623–1840*, p. 236. For a full discussion of this approach to plotting in the comedies, see Bertrand Evans, *Shakespeare's Comedies* (Oxford, 1960).

7. For the possibility that Lady Macbeth is feigning, see Irene Dash, *Women's Worlds in Shakespeare's Plays* (Newark, 1997), p.173ff.

8. See Ernest Schanzer, "The Structural Pattern of *The Winter's Tale*," *Review of English Literature* 5:2 (1964), 72–82.

9. If, as some scholars argue, Shakespeare created this work on commission as a part of the marriage festivities for an aristocratic family, then *A Midsummmer Night's Dream* would be a play written and performed to celebrate a wedding that contains in its enactment a play, *Pyramus and Thisby*, written and performed to celebrate a wedding.

10. Bernard McElroy, *Shakespeare's Mature Tragedies* (Princeton, 1973), p.157.

11. G. M. Pinciss, "The Old Honor and the New Courtesy: *1 Henry IV*," *Shakespeare Survey* 31 (1978), 85–91.

12. M. M. Mahood, *Shakespeare's Wordplay*, (London, 1957).

13. Janet Adelman, *The Common Liar: An Essay on "Antony and Cleopatra"* (New Haven, 1973), p.31.

14. Mark Rose, *Shakespearean Design* (Cambridge, 1972), pp.96–98.

15. Rose, pp.154–57.

16. Rose, pp.144–47.

17. Stanley Wells, "Shakespeare and Romance," in *Later Shakespeare,* ed. John Russell Brown and Bernard Harris (London, 1966), pp.49–79.

18. Norman Rabkin, *Shakespeare and the Problem of Meaning* (Chicago, 1981), pp.36–62.

19. Ernest Jones, *Hamlet and Oedipus* (New York, 1949).

20. Harry Levin, *The Question of Hamlet* (New York, 1959).

21. Daniel C. Boughner, *The Braggart in Renaissance Comedy* (Minneapolis, 1954).

22. Bernard Spivack, *Shakespeare and the Allegory of Evil* (New York, 1958).

23. See J. Dover Wilson, *The Fortunes of Falstaff* (New York, 1943).

24. Enid Welsford, *The Fool: His Social and Literary History* (London, 1935).

25. G. M. Pinciss, *Literary Creations: Conventional Characters in the Drama of Shakespeare and His Contemporaries* (Woodbridge, 1988), pp.14–24.

26. Samuel Coleridge, *Lectures, "Othello," in Shakespeare Criticism 1623–1840*, ed. D. Nichol Smith, p.268.

27. McElroy, p.155ff.

28. Helge Kokeritz, *Shakespeare's Pronunciation* (New Haven, 1953), pp.58–59.

29. G. M. Pinciss, *Shakespeare's World* (New York, 1989), Chapter IV.

30. See G. M. Pinciss, "Rhetoric as Character: The Forum Speeches in *Julius Caesar*," *The Upstart Crow* IV (Fall, 1982), pp.113–119 for a more detailed account of this scene.

31. Brian Vickers, *The Artistry of Shakespeare's Prose* (London, 1968).

32. See William C. Carroll, *The Great Feast of Language in Love's Labour's Lost* (Princeton, 1976). My remarks on this play are greatly indebted to this fine study.

33. Richmond Noble, *Shakespeare's Biblical Knowledge* (London, 1935).

34. *"On Sitting Down to Read King Lear Once Again."*

35. Anne Righter (Barton), *Shakespeare and the Idea of the Play* (Harmondsworth, 1967).

36. Anne Barton, *Essays, Mainly Shakespearean* (Cambridge, 1994), pp.91–112.

37. Paul A. Cantor, *Shakespeare Hamlet* (New York, 1989), p.57ff.

38. John Wilders, *The Lost Garden: Shakespeare's English and Roman History Plays* (Totowa, 1978), 102ff.

39. Lectures on the English Poets in *Shakespeare Criticism 1623–1840*, ed. D. Nichol Smith, p. 306.

40. Bernard Beckerman, *Shakespeare at the Globe* (New York, 1962), p. 9.

41. Andrew Gurr, *The Shakespearean Stage, 1574–1642* (Cambridge, 1970), p.82ff.

42. Andrew Gurr, *Playgoing in Shakespeare's London* (New York, 1987), p.63ff.

43. Jonathan Bate, *The Genius of Shakespeare* (London, 1997), p.294ff.

44. Stanley Wells ed., *A Midsummer Night's Dream*, (Harmondsworth, 1967), p.10.

45. R. A. Foakes ed., *A Midsummer Night's Dream* (Cambridge, 1984), pp.13–14.

46. The film was released in London in November, 1944, and "became the most successful British film in history running uninterrupted for eleven months," p.182. Its American premier was in April, 1946. Donald Spoto, *Laurence Olivier, A Biography* (New York, 1992).

INDEX

All page numbers in italic refer to illustrations.